Urban Social Work

URBAN SOCIAL WORK

A.K. Patel
M.V. Dubey

CRESCENT
PUBLISHING CORPORATION

[The responsibility for the facts stated, conclusions reached and plagiarism, if any, in this book is entirely that of the Author. And the Publisher bears no responsibility for them, whatsoever.]

Urban Social Work

First Published : 2010

ISBN 978-81-8342-174-4

Published by :

CRESCENT PUBLISHING CORPORATION
4831/24, Prahlad Street,
Ansari Road, Darya Ganj,
New Delhi - 110002
Ph. : 23272541, 23257835
Fax : 91- 011- 23257835
e-mail : campusbooks@hotmail.com
commonwealth_pub@yahoo.com

Laser Typesetting by :
Anupama Computers
Delhi

Printed at :
Roshan Offset Printers
Delhi

Preface

Urban is an area where economic activity, politics, social, law, culture and other type of activity concentrate altogether in a specific and unique spatial arrangement. Various issues arisen from these activities convergences, such as transportation, congestion, pollution, poverty, crime, health, education, public service provision, taxation, urban environment, and others. Ideas of how to solve these problems vary as well. Urban social problems are considered to require an integrative approach and collaboration between social workers and other parties such as care workers, police, citizen's organisations and private business.

The problems in urban settings demand an increasingly broad mix of academic and professional skills. This book is designed to equip tomorrow's leading social professionals, policy makers, researchers, public sector managers, and advisors with the mix of insights and skills they will need. It aims to study the ways in which social problems in urban areas are defined and solved, and analyses the roles ascribed to professionals in these processes. By reading this book, students will acquire academic knowledge, professional attitudes, and research skills needed to play an active and/or research role in this field.

A.K. Patel
M.V. Dubey

Contents

1

Social Problems of Urban Settings

Increasing levels of urbanisation are caused by natural growth of the urban population and migration of the rural population towards cities. Over the past halfcentury, a great rural-to-urban population shift has occurred and the process of urbanisation (the concentration of people and activities into areas classified as urban) is set to continue well into the 21st century. Driving forces include the opportunities and services offered in urban areas — especially jobs and education — while in some parts of the world, notably Africa, conflict, land degradation and exhaustion of natural resources are also important.

Cities play a major role not only as providers of employment, shelter and services but also as centres of culture, learning and technological development, portals to the rest of the world, industrial centres for the processing of agricultural produce and manufacturing, and places to generate income.

There is a strong positive link between national levels of human development and urbanisation levels. However, the implications of rapid urban growth include increasing unemployment, environmental degradation, lack of urban services, overburdening of existing infrastructure and lack of access to land, finance and adequate shelter. Managing the urban environment sustainably will therefore become one of the major challenges for the future.

Levels of urbanisation are closely correlated with national income — the more developed countries are already mostly urbanised — and in almost every country, urban areas account for a disproportionate share of the gross national product (GNP). Bangkok, for example, produces 40 per cent of Thailand's output, whereas only 12 per cent of its population lives in this city. Worldwide, cities produce on average 60 per cent of a country's GNP. The rapid increase of the world's urban population coupled with the slowing of rural population growth has led to a major redistribution of the population over the past 30 years. By 2007, one-half of the world's population will live in urban areas compared to little more than one-third in 1972, and the period 1950 to 2050 will see a shift from a 65 per cent rural population to 65 per cent urban. By 2002, some 70 per cent of the world's urban population will be living in Africa, Asia or Latin America.

The most striking current changes are the levels of urbanisation in less developed nations: rising from about 27 per cent in 1975 to 40 per cent in 2000 — an increase of more than 1 200 million people. Furthermore, there is every indication that the trend will continue for the next 30 years, adding 2 000 million people to the urban population of the presently less-developed nations. Within these global averages, there are complex regional differences in urban growth and change. The annual percentage change in the urban population by region shows a general slowing in the rate of urbanisation for all regions except North America.

There has been a dramatic increase in the number and size of megacities and urban agglomerations in the second half of the 20th century, as well as a change in the geographical distribution of these cities: in 1900, nine of the ten largest cities were in North America and Europe, whereas today only three are located in the developed world. However, most of the world's urban population still lives in small and medium-sized cities which, in most countries, are now growing faster than the very large cities.

Globalisation has been progressing for decades but under the impact of new information technologies the speed of globalisation has quickened and its reach has broadened. These technologies are reinforcing the importance of knowledge and information in economic transformation, while reducing the relative importance of traditional manufacturing and industrial development based on raw materials.

In urban areas, this has manifested itself in the growth of the service sector in both absolute and relative terms. Technology has increased the already dominant economic role and importance of urban areas, not just those in the more developed economies but globally, indicating the growing importance of cities in the global economy. In India, software development and related information-communication services is the leading sector for economic growth. This new growth sector — which has grown more rapidly and become internationally more competitive than any of the country's traditional industrial sectors — is concentrated in large urban areas because of the superior infrastructure and educational levels of human resources offered by cities.

In the 1970s, a new phase of globalisation started with the deregulation of labour markets, liberalisation of financial markets, and privatisation of government functions. One of the results was increasing competition for foreign direct investment and employers found themselves able to shift the location of their production facilities more easily, which worsened job and income security in some urban areas but benefited others.

Between the 1970s and mid-1990s, some Asian countries clearly benefited from this development and showed spectacular economic growth and growth in general well-being. However, during 1997–98 the economic crisis in Asia struck not only these economies but also some in other regions. The human impacts of the crisis were severe; poverty in Asia increased and there were massive lay-offs, particularly of women, the young and the unskilled.

The Asian crisis showed that urban areas are highly vulnerable to global economic impacts. Although globalisation has often increased opportunities for jobs and knowledge, it has also increased social inequalities and poverty. Benefits are not equally shared, resulting in large groups of people living in slums in developing countries unconnected to water and sanitary services, and unemployment, poor health and social exclusion in the developed world.

Urban poverty

Poverty is among the major drivers of environmental degradation. The urban poor, who are unable to compete for scarce resources or protect themselves from harmful environmental conditions, are most affected by the negative impacts of urbanisation. The growth of large cities, particularly in developing countries, has been accompanied by an increase in urban poverty which tends to be concentrated in certain social groups and in particular locations. Causes include an increasing gap between incomes and land prices, and the failure of housing markets to provide for low-income groups. Land development processes tend to serve middle and higher income classes, forcing the poor to settle in high densities on marginal lands within cities or in the urban periphery, sometimes in areas at risk from environmental hazards such as floods and landslides, and without access to basic services such as water and sanitation.

Urban poverty is on the increase. It is estimated that one-quarter of the population lives below the poverty line and that female-headed households are disproportionately affected. Worldwide, there is a clear correlation between their poverty and lack of control over resources and lack of full citizenship.

Urban Environment

Urban areas do not have only local environmental impacts but also large so-called 'ecological footprints'. In their immediate vicinity, cities have a variety of impacts: conversion of agricultural or forest land for urban uses and infrastructure, reclaiming of wetlands, quarrying and excavation of sand, gravel and building materials in large quantities and, in some regions, deforestation to meet fuel demand.

The use of biomass fuel also causes indoor and outdoor air pollution. Other effects can be felt further afield such as pollution of waterways, lakes and coastal waters by untreated effluent. Air pollution from cities has an impact on residents' health as well as on vegetation and soils at a considerable distance. Urban transport contributes to air pollution and the large concentration of cars and industries in cities causes the lion's share of urban global greenhouse gas emissions.

Cities are often located in prime agricultural areas. If this land is converted for urban uses, this puts additional pressure on nearby areas that may be less suitable for agriculture. Urbanisation in coastal areas often leads to the destruction of sensitive ecosystems and can also alter the hydrology of coasts and their natural features such as mangrove swamps, reefs and beaches that serve as barriers to erosion and form important habitats for species.

Low to medium density residential areas around urban centres are common in the developed world. Well developed infrastructure and the increasing use of the car have facilitated this trend. Urban sprawl has an especially damaging effect on the environment associated with the increase in use of private motorised transport. Furthermore, low density development occupies proportionally larger areas of land per capita.

Water is a key issue in urban areas. The intensity of demand in cities can quickly exceed local supply. The price of water is typically lower than the actual cost of obtaining, treating and distributing it, partly because of government subsidies. As a result, households and industries have little incentive to contaminated land management.

Another problem emerging in developed countries is the lack of suitable landfill sites to cater for the increasing demand for solid waste disposal. Worsening environmental conditions can have serious effects on human health and welfare, particularly for the poor. Poor sanitation creates environmental and health hazards particularly by direct exposure to faeces and drinking water conserve water. Pollution from urban run-off, sewage and untreated discharges of industries has adversely affected many water bodies, leaving many cities with unsafe water supply.

Although local environmental problems tend to diminish with increasing income levels, other environmental problems tend to become worse. The most obvious are high levels of energy use and increasing levels of consumption and waste production. Urban residents rely heavily on fossil fuels and electricity, and wealthy cities tend to use more energy and produce more waste.

Inadequate waste collection and waste management systems are the cause of serious urban pollution and health hazards, especially in cities in developing countries. Cities in industrialised countries are now also facing the consequences of past environmentally damaging production techniques and inadequate waste disposal. This has resulted in many different forms of pollution and in particular the formation of brownfields: abandoned, vacant or underused former industrial areas where redevelopment is hampered by environmental problems and lack of adequate information on contamination.

Air and water pollution cause chronic and infectious respiratory disease, water-borne diseases such as diarrhoea and intestinal worm infections, increased mortality rates particularly among children and premature deaths – especially among the poor. However, worldwide epidemiological and demographic information suggests that survival rates are better in cities than in rural areas because of better access to health services.

The urban poor are particularly exposed because of their location and because they have limited resources with which to compensate for these problems by buying potable water, securing medical care or escaping floods. There are many other less quantifiable but nonetheless important environmental impacts, such as loss of green space in urban areas, destruction of special local ecosystems, noise pollution, and aesthetically unpleasant sights and smells. These not only constitute a genuine loss of well-being but they can also erode civic pride and lower morale, leading to indifference and cynicism locally and to a negative image externally.

The relatively disproportionate urban environmental footprint is acceptable to a certain extent because, for some issues, the per capita environmental impact of cities is smaller than would be made by a similar number of people in a rural setting. Cities concentrate populations in a way that reduces land pressure and provides economies of scale and proximity of infrastructure and services. Urban areas therefore hold promise for sustainable development because of their ability to support a large number of people while limiting their per capita impact on the natural environment.

Environmental problems occur because of the concentration of environmentally negative impacts. Good urban planning can reduce these impacts. Wellplanned, densely populated settlements can reduce the need for land conversion, provide opportunities for energy savings and make recycling more costeffective. If cities are properly managed, with adequate attention paid to social development and the environment, the problems present as a result of rapid urbanisation, particularly in developing regions, can be avoided.

/A first step in this direction would be for national governments to incorporate a clear urban component in their economic and other policies. Successes in urban environmental management include increases in resource efficiency, reductions in waste generation, improving urban infrastructure for water supply, the management and conservation of water resources in urban areas by improved waste water treatment and through legislation, setting up of recycling schemes, development of more effective waste collection systems, strict legislation for the treatment of hazardous waste, waste collection through public-private partnership, adoption of energy technologies by industry and households, and restoration of brownfields.

URBAN GOVERNANCE

Many urban environmental problems are the result of poor management, poor planning and absence of coherent urban policies rather than of urbanisation itself. Through experience, it has been learned that no amount of finance, technology or expertise can secure environmentally sustainable development — or protect the environment — if the fundamentals of governance are not participatory, democratic and pluralistic. For example, many developing countries have extensive regulations on pollution, most of which are seldom if ever applied effectively because of the lack of proper institutions, legal systems, political will and competent governance. Unfortunately, particularly where economic and social change is rapid, established political and administrative institutions have proved highly resistant to change.

The past 30 years have seen significant political change with profound implications for urban areas and for the urban and global environment. These include:

- the collapse of central planning;
- the extension of democracy;
- decentralisation and demands for empowerment and self-determination;
- increasing pluralism in politics and society; and
- pressures for participation, accountability and transparency in government.

These trends appear to be strengthening, reinforced by globalisation and especially by the impact of freer and faster flows of information and knowledge. Efforts to improve urban governance involve activities such as promoting participatory processes; developing effective partnerships with and among all actors of civil society, particularly the private and community sectors; securing greater effective empowerment of local government, including greater autonomy in finance and legislation; and reform of unresponsive organisations and bureaucratic structures.

They also involve city-to-city cooperation and exchange of experiences and lessons learned. The International Council for Local Environmental Initiatives works with 286 local governments in 43 countries to improve local energy management and reduce greenhouse gas emissions. Initiatives such as the Stockholm Partnership for Sustainable Cities have been developed to introduce sustainability into city planning through partnership between cities and business. Habitat's Local Agenda 21 initiatives have been proved effective in implementing sustainable development policies that involve community members and government.

Because of the importance of specific local circumstances and political realities, there is no viable approach to solving urban environmental problems that can be applied in every city. A first step is to develop a local environmental agenda to assess the local situation regarding environmental issues so that this information can be used in city planning. Whereas the emphasis in 1970 was largely focused on public policy and regulation, the focus of the early 1990s was on markets and technical solutions. At the turn of the century, urban environmental management appears to be focusing more on changing cultures — corporate, economic and political.

Social Problems of African Urban Areas

While the majority of the African population is still rural, urban growth rates at nearly 4 per cent a year are the most rapid in the world, and nearly twice the global average . Growth rates are predicted to average 3.5 per cent per year over the next 15 years, meaning that Africa's share of the world's urban population will increase from 10 to 17 per cent between 2000 and 2015.

North Africa is the most urbanised sub-region with an average urban population of 54 per cent, followed by West Africa (40 per cent), Southern Africa (39 per cent), Central Africa (36 per cent) and the Western Indian Ocean islands (32 per cent). The least urbanised sub-region is Eastern Africa with only 23 per cent of the population living in urban areas. Malawi has the highest urban growth rate of any country in Africa, which at 6.3 per cent is three times the world rate. Not only are there more people living in cities but the cities themselves are becoming larger, and more numerous.

There are now 43 cities in Africa with populations of more than one million inhabitants, a figure which is expected to increase to almost 70 by 2015. Africa's high urban growth rate is a result of ruralurban migration, population growth and, in some areas, conflict. People leave rural areas because of declining agricultural productivity, lack of employment opportunities and lack of access to basic physical and social infrastructure.

The expectation of higher incomes and standards of living in urban areas is seldom realised, however, and urban poverty is widespread and growing. In Moroni, Comoros, 40 per cent of the population lives in poverty, and in Southern Africa up to 45 per cent of urban households grow crops or raise livestock in urban environments in order to supplement their livelihoods. Environmental disasters and conflicts have also caused many people to flee rural areas and seek refuge in urban centres. In Mozambique, about 4.5 million rural people were displaced to urban areas due to civil strife in the 1980s, while the third largest settlement in Sierra Leone is a displaced persons camp.

Because of slow economic growth in many African countries, lack of sound development policies and an increasing number of small households, infrastructure development has been unable to keep pace with the burgeoning need for shelter and services for growing urban populations. As a result, many African cities have an increasing number of overcrowded, informal settlements, or 'shanty towns', characterised by inadequate housing and poor provision of infrastructure such as roads, street lights, water supplies, sanitation and waste management services. Often these settlements are developed on fragile environments such as steep slopes, natural drainage waterways and flood-prone areas. Inadequate housing and settlement design can also contribute to declining security and increasing levels of crime in African cities.

Governments and authorities have attempted to meet the demand for housing and services through increased construction. South Africa, for example, has produced more than one million low-cost houses during the past six years. However, lack of awareness of resource-efficient construction practices has resulted in excessive use of natural resources and generation of large amounts of construction waste that is rarely recycled. In addition, new settlements have mostly been on open land on the urban periphery rather than on little used land within the cities, thus requiring expansion of infrastructure rather than more intensive use of existing networks. Attention is now shifting to integrated development planning, and housing policies that support environmentally sustainable housing have been developed in some countries.

Key environmental issues in urban areas in Africa are related to the provision of services for waste, water and sanitation, and urban air pollution.

Water Supply and Sanitation

The volume of solid waste generated in urban areas is increasing with the growing population, higher consumption levels and the use of more packaging in the retail industry. Rates of waste generation are outstripping the capacities of local authorities to collect, treat and dispose of waste. Across Africa, only 31 per cent of solid wastes in urban areas are collected.

Inadequate urban infrastructure leads to untreated waste and waste remaining uncollected or improperly disposed of. In Accra, for example, although there is a system of collection from waste points in most residential areas, collection is erratic and legal intermediary dumps overflow. Burning of solid waste is common in many countries but the toxic fumes thus released contribute to air pollution. Only 2 per cent of African waste is recovered and recycled due to lack of economic incentives and markets for recycled materials. The most commonly recycled materials are paper, textiles, glass, plastic and metal. Composting is carried out to some extent in Egypt, Morocco and Tunisia.

The proliferation of unplanned settlements in the urban areas of Africa has been accompanied by inadequate provision of potable water and sanitation. On average, 85 per cent of African urban populations had access to improved water sources in the year 2000, although this ranged from 100 per cent in Botswana, Djibouti, Mauritius, Morocco and Namibia, to just 29 per cent in Guinea-Bissau and 31 per cent in Chad. The average urban population with access to improved sanitation was 84 per cent, ranging from 100 per cent in Mauritius and Morocco to 12 per cent in Rwanda and 14 per cent in Congo. The numbers of people with these services have increased over the past 10 years but the percentages have hardly changed.

In order to improve the performance of municipal governments and public utilities, public-private partnerships are being increasingly promoted to provide water management and sanitation services. These partnerships have met with mixed success. While private participation in water supply and sanitation services brings in new investment capital, management and organisational skills, and technical know-how, there is a perceived bias towards meeting the demands of upper and middle-income groups.

Air Pollution

A growing concern in many urban centres, particularly large cities, is the level of air pollution, mainly from vehicle exhausts, industrial emissions, and domestic use of woodfuel, coal, paraffin and refuse for heating and cooking. In Cairo, fumes from the 1.2 million vehicles, combined with suspended particulate matter and sand blown into urban areas from the neighbouring desert create an almost permanent haze over the city. Levels of suspended particulate matter and lead pollution are among the highest in the world, creating a high risk of respiratory disorders to the 10.6 million inhabitants. In recognition of this risk, only unleaded fuel is now sold in Cairo, and the rest of the country is expected to follow suit by the end of 2002.

In dense, informal settlements, the use of traditional fuel sources contributes to rising ambient levels of sulphur dioxide, nitrogen oxides, carbon monoxide, ozone and suspended particulate matter. Exposure to these pollutants is associated with increased risk of acute respiratory infections, particularly among children. Electrification of households, promotion of low-smoke fuels, and improved ventilation of houses are some of the measures that have been adopted to reduce health risks.

Problems of Urban Areas in Asia and the Pacific

Urbanisation in Asia and the Pacific is predicted to grow at an average rate of 2.4 per cent per annum between 2001 and 2015. The current level of urbanisation ranges from a low of 7.1 per cent in Bhutan to 100 per cent in Singapore and Nauru. Australia and New Zealand is the most urbanised subregion (85 per cent) and South Pacific the least (26.4 per cent).

In seven countries in the region (Australia, Japan, Nauru, New Caledonia, New Zealand, Republic of Korea and Singapore) the level of urbanisation is more than 75 per cent, while the 12 megacities in the region — Beijing, Calcutta, Delhi, Dhaka, Jakarta, Karachi, Metro Manila, Mumbai, Osaka, Seoul, Shanghai and Tokyo — accommodate 12 per cent of the urban population.

In some of the larger cities, excluding those in Australia and New Zealand, up to 60 per cent of the inhabitants live in informal settlements, with a population density of up to 2 500 persons per hectare. These settlements suffer from a lack of infrastructure and services such as water supplies, sewerage, drainage, roads, health care and education. The major urban environmental issues in the region are air pollution and inadequate services.

Urban Air Pollution

Air pollution is common, particularly in developing country cities, due to the growing number of motor vehicles and increasing industrial activity. In countries such as India, Indonesia, Nepal, Malaysia and Thailand vehicles with two-stroke engines, such as motorcycles and three-wheel taxis, comprise more than one-half of all motor traffic and pollute heavily. Poor maintenance of vehicles, poor fuel quality and poor road conditions also contribute. The burning of biomass such as firewood and agricultural wastes is a further source of air pollution in many poor areas. Motor vehicles cause serious environmental problems in developed countries as well. In Australia and New Zealand, there is a high dependence on private motor vehicles which leads not only to the need to clear land for roads but also to increasing emissions of carbon dioxide, lead, zinc and copper.

A range of policy measures and technologies including catalytic converters, unleaded fuel and alternative fuels such as compressed natural gas are being introduced to improve the quality of urban air. New coal-fired power plants in many Asian countries now use electrostatic precipitators which can reduce emissions of particulates by more than 99 per cent. Subsidies are provided for the use of renewable technologies such as wind turbines and solar photovoltaics. In China, the city of Beijing has implemented 68 atmospheric pollution prevention measures which are resulting in significant reductions in SO2, NO2 and SPM levels.

Waste Management

Much of the solid waste generated in urban centres remains uncollected and is either deposited in surface waters and empty lots, or burned in streets. This problem has worsened over the past 30 years. Collected waste is mainly disposed of in open dumps, many of which are neither properly operated nor maintained, and which pose a serious threat to public health. Only a few Asian cities such as Hong Kong and Singapore, and those in Australia, Japan and New Zealand, have adequate solid waste disposal facilities but even these cities have problems in dealing with increasing volumes of waste. In the mid-1990s, Metro Manila generated 6 300 tonnes of solid waste daily but its landfills could accommodate only a little more than half that amount. The island of Kiribati has severe population density problems caused by internal migration and has little land for waste disposal. As on many atoll islands, solid waste is discharged into coastal waters.

Serious health and environmental problems can be caused by poor waste disposal. In the Pacific Islands, freshwater is scarce, and solid waste disposal methods that contaminate water are frequently a source of intestinal diseases and ear and eye infections. In India, an outbreak of bubonic plague in 1994 was linked to inadequate solid waste disposal. The disposal and treatment of industrial, toxic and hazardous waste also causes serious problems. Dumping of hazardous waste is common in South and Southeast Asia.

Countries such as Bangladesh, India and Pakistan have become dumping grounds for significant quantities of hazardous waste from industrialised countries, and are facing growing protests about waste-related pollution. A large number of stakeholders are involved in national waste management policies and strategies. Waste management services have been privatised in countries such as Japan, the Republic of Korea, Malaysia and Thailand. This appears to be an effective means of improving these services, while providing additional employment. However, much waste is generated by small producers, who are difficult to service with traditional methods.

Water and Sanitation

For most cities, providing an adequate and safe supply of water for domestic and industrial uses is a major problem. In spite of significant investments, the sewage systems in many major cities still cannot support a high-density urban environment with the result that sewage is often discharged directly to drains or waterways, or disposed of in individual septic tanks that are poorly maintained. Afghanistan has by far the lowest percentage of urban population with access to improved water sources (19 per cent) and sanitation (25 per cent) in the region. However, in absolute terms China and India have by far the largest number of urban people (more than 20 million each) without access to a safe water supply. Sanitation services are less developed than water supply, with 23 per cent of urban residents still lacking adequate sanitation (compared to only 7 per cent lacking access to improved water sources). These figures are compiled from the sample of 38 Asian and Pacific countries for which statistics are available for the year 2000.

More than 50 per cent of the urban population in Afghanistan and Mongolia still have no access to improved sanitation. Another major urban environmental issue is flooding and land subsidence. For example, in Bangkok monsoon run-off frequently exceeds the Chao Phraya river drainage capacity — a problem exacerbated by the progressive filling of the 'khlongs' (canals) as urban areas expand. Furthermore, excessive groundwater extraction has produced remarkable land subsidence in Bangkok. Land subsidence increases the probability and worsens the impacts of flooding. Similar conditions are reported in other river basins.

Addressing Environmental Problems

Several governments are promoting decentralised and participatory development to help mobilise resources for improving urban infrastructure. However, the process of decentralisation is severely constrained by a lack of institutional capacity among local governments, limited resource mobilisation at the local level, and limited access to long-term financing for investment programmes. Although decentralisation and local autonomy are gaining more momentum, excessive controls are still exercised by higher levels of governments resulting in a mismatch between the responsibilities of local governments and their resources. In addition to national actions, international and regional programmes have been developed to support urban environmental management in the region. These include the Regional Action Plan on Urbanisation, Asia-Pacific Initiative 2000, Land Management Programme, the Local Leadership and Management Training Programme, and Action Planning for Sustainable Urban Development.

Urbanisation is one of the most significant issues facing Asia and the Pacific. Uncontrolled growth, inappropriate waste disposal practices, lack of adequate drinking water supply and sanitation facilities, flooding and land subsidence are crucial issues facing urban areas today. In response, investment in domestic wastewater systems, solid waste management schemes, and water supply schemes have been accelerated in many countries. Urban areas offer opportunities for employment, better education and health facilities but they find it increasingly difficult to provide the physical infrastructure required for adequate services to underpin human health and well-being.

2

Urban Social Welfare

The aim of social service in the past was essentially curative, and efforts were directed towards relief for the handicapped and the uplift of the under-privileged sections of society. It is now essential to maintain vigilance over weaknesses and strains in the social structure and to provide against them by organising social services. The aim of all social work now has to be the gradual rehabilitation of all weak, handicapped and anti-social elements in society.

Some of the important social problems like poverty, ignorance, over-population and rural backwardness are of a general nature and, in varying degree, they are influenced by factors like squalor and bad housing, malnutrition and physical and mental ill- health, neglected childhood, family disorganisation and a low standard of living.

For a long time, society has remained apathetic to these conditions; but with the awakening of political consciousness and the enthusiasm of organisations and workers to improve social conditions, there is a possibility of developing programmes which could gradually remedy the present situation. The economic programmes of the Five Year Plan will mitigate these problems to some extent, but the gains of economic development have to be maintained and consolidated by well-conceived and organised social welfare programmes spread over the entire country.

The principal social welfare problems relate to women, children, youth, the family, under-privileged groups and social vice. The social health of any community will depend a great deal upon the status, functions and responsibilities of the woman in the family and in the community. Social conditions should give to the woman opportunities for creative selfexpression, so that she can make her full contribution towards the economic and social life of the community.

Some problems of women have to be dealt through social legislation, but other problems pertaining to health, social education., vocational training, increased participation in social and cultural life, provision of shelter, and assistance to the handicapped or maladjusted call for programmes at the community level.

As women have to fulfil heavy domestic and economic responsibilities, adequate attention has to be paid to the need for relaxation and recreation both in the homes as well as in the community. The welfare agencies have catered to some extent to the needs of the widow and the destitute woman, but the quality of the service rendered by them and the nature of their work needs to be surveyed.

Considering the numbers involved, the needs of children should receive much greater consideration than is commonly given to them. There is a growing demand for child health services and educational facilities. The standard of child welfare services in the country can be improved if the rate of increase in population is reduced. Malnutrition is perhaps the major cause of ill-health and lack of proper growth of the child. The feeding of the child in the early years is the responsibility of the family, and is dependent upon economic conditions and traditional food habits. The nature and extent of malnutrition has to be determined, and resources have to be found to supplement and improve the diet of children through schools and community and child welfare agencies.

The problem of children's recreation and development outside educational institutions has received some attention during recent years, but play activities of children are considerably restricted in urban areas on account of the environmental conditions, lack of adequate space, and, to some extent, neglect of this vital need of the child by the family and the community. Not enough is known about the work of private agencies for the welfare of destitute and homeless children.

The juvenile courts and children's aid societies have so far touched a fringe of the problem of children's welfare. Certain special aspects may be briefly mentioned. The existing facilities for handicapped and deficient children are far from adequate and suitable agencies have to be created. Hospitals provide treatment for polio, congenital deformities, fractures, bone disorders and other diseases, but there is a need to extend existing services and provide special institutions and care for disabled and crippled children.

At present deficient children attend educational institutions together with normal children and seldom receive treatment and special training to enable them to overcome their handicaps. The subject needs to be studied carefully. The problem of juvenile delinquency has already received considerable attention and many of the States have special legislation. juvenile delinquency may often be the result of poverty and many offences may be traced to the connivance or support of adults.

The youth constitute the most vital section of the community. In recent years, young people have had to fact and have been increasingly conscious of problems such as inadequate educational facilities, unemployment, and lack of apportunity for social development, national service and leadership. The problems of health, education and employment of youth have been considered a aspects of national problems in these fields.

Social welfare is primarily concerned with the improvement of services provided for the benefit of youth by welfare agencies with the object of promoting development of character and training for citizenship and for physical, interllectual and moral fitness. It is necessary to encourage initiative among youth so that though their own organisations, they can develop programmes of youth welfare and national service. Ways must also be found to give opportunities to youth for active participation in constructive activity. Such training and experience will equip them for shouldering the responsibilities of leadership in different spheres of national life.

Traditionally, the family has been left largely to its own resources to deal with most of its problems, although in some cases it may be assisted by the larger community groups (such as caste) to which a family may belong. Questions relating to status and rights, property, inheritance, etc., are the subject of social legislation. The gradual break-up of the joint family and the emergence of the small family has increased its economic problems and burdens. Family responsibilities have now to be borne at a comparatively younger age by the head of the small family than happended in the joint family. This creasing complexity of the social situation and handicaps arising from physical disability, ailment or unemployment render it more difficult for the family to8 provide a sense of security to its members. This fact suggests a number of problems which, along with other problems studied carefully if welfare agencies are to develop suitable methods of treatment for guiding and assisting those in need.

There are number of under-privileged communities such as the scheduled tribes, scheduled castes and other backward classes including criminal tribes. The problems of poverty, ill-health, and lack of opportunities for development affect them to a larger extent than many other sections of the society.

Every community has its share of those who are physically handicapped such as the blind, the deaf and dumb, and those who are crippled and infirm. Reliable statistics are not available about the extent of the population which suffers from such handicaps. A certain number of welfare agencies are already working in this field, but little information about their resources and their ability to deal with the problem is at present available.

The main problems to be considered under the description of social vice are prostitution, crime and delinquency, alcoholism, gambling and beggary. These problems have existed for a long period, although necessarily their nature and extent vary according to the prevailing social and economic conditions. Some of them have to be dealt with largely by local communities, and the approach and treatment have to be varied from place to place.

The character, and magnitude of these problems of social defence have to be determined carefully before the value and efficacy of the existing agencies and programmes could be assessed. Social legislation deals with many, of the social evils with a view to controlling and even eradicating them, but its actual implementation-needs to be watched. Among the practical problems to be resolved are the demarcation of the relative roles of State and private agencies, determination of the machinery of enforcement, estimation of the resources required, examination of methods, development of correct programmes, and creation of public opinion in favour of an objective and dispassionate approach to the problems of social vice.

SOCIAL WELFARE AGENCIES

As the social structure becomes more complex, the State is called upon to play an increasing role in providing services for the welfare of the people. The Central Government, the various State Governments and local self-governing bodies, each in its own sphere, have to ensure that they have at least the minimum administrative machinery for dealing with social problems. What form this machinery takes will depend on their particular circumstances find requirements, but it is certain that without the necessary machinery they will not be able to pursue their programmes.

The functions of the social welfare machinery of the Central and State Governments may, for instance, be:-

(1) to study the need for and the efficacy of social legislation,

(2) to execute programmes of social welfare,

(3) to assist, both directly and through other agencies, the development of social services, the study of social problems, and the creation of trained personnel for social administration,

(4) to assist specialised and private agencies through guidance, and financially, and to protect the interest of society by a measure of regulation and control,

(5) to initiate pilot projects, or help field organisations to develop such projects, in order to demonstrate the

efficacy of programmes, methods, leadership and organisation,

(6) to promote initiative in and improvement of social services by supplying information, materials, publications, audio-visual aids, etc., and

(7) to take over social services of vital importance initiated and organised by private agencies when these develop beyond their ability to manage.

Local self-governing bodies can do much to co-ordinate welfare activities in their areas and promote co-operation between their departments and the work of private agencies. Local committees or councils of social service agencies could undertake activities such as the following depending upon the resources which are available or can be raised

(a) taking effective measures to alleviate suffering, especially by providing emergency relief

(b) organising and assisting community centres

(c) improving housing conditions, clearing slums and providing welfare services and special amenities for communities residing in slum areas;

(d) promoting child welfare activities

(e) providing parks, playgrounds and other amenities for physical recreation and welfare

(f) supporting private social service agencies and institutions for social education, women's welfare, youth welfare, aid welfare of handicapped persons and underprivileged communities; and

(g) creating public opinion and assisting the vigilance authorities in the control of social vice and beggary.

The interrelationship between the various activities has to be emphasised and the necessary co-ordination assured both in the Central Government and in the States. One aspect of this coordination would be to secure that legislation relating to social problems follows broadly similar principles. In cases where grants-in-aid are given by a State authority to a private agency, it is desirable to lay down general directions for improving the content of the programmes and their administration. A measure of supervision and inspection should also be provided in order to maintain standards of efficiency.

A major responsibility for organising activities in different fields of social welfare, like the welfare of women and children, social education, community organisation, etc., falls naturally on private voluntary agencies. These private agencies have for long been working in their own humble way and without adequate State aid for the achievement of their objectives; with their own leadership, Organisation and resources.

Any plan for the social and economic regeneration of the country should take into account the service rendered by these private agencies and the State should give them the maximum co-operation in strengthening their efforts. Public co-operation, through these voluntary social service organisations, is capable of yielding valuable results in canalising private effort for the promotion of social welfare.

One of the most important tasks of the State is to conduct a Survey of the nature, quality and extent of service rendered by voluntary agencies in different parts of the country, to assess the extent of financial and other aid that they are in need of in order to develop their programmes of work, and to coordinate their activities. A sum of Rs. 4 crores has been provided as grants-in-aid to voluntary social service organisations for strengthening, improving and extending the existing activities in the field of social welfare and for developing new programmes and carrying out pilot projects. It is envisaged that this fund of Rs. 4 crores should be administered by a board to be set up by the Central Government to which a great deal of administrative authority will be devolved, The board Should be predominently composed of non-officials who have actual experience of field work in promoting voluntary welfare activities.

It is necessary to co-ordinate the programmes of various agencies so as to guide them into broad streams and bring added strength and intensity of purpose to welfare activities. Such co- ordination calls for a common approach and a co-operative outlook on the part of the organisers of voluntary social work. Further, it will be necessary to induce agencies to agree to subordinate their individual interests to some extent and thus make collective effort possible not merely in the execution of programmes, but also in the economic and rational use of personnel. Such co-operation could also lead to joint effort in obtaining resources.

Co-ordination need not involve on the part of the co-operating organisations loss of individuality or of freedom to organise and to carry out programmes. Co-ordination will have to be of two types-. In the first place, there may be functional co-ordination on the part of national organisations striving to achieve specific objectives like physical fitness, child welfare, youth welfare, social education, community Organisation, etc. Secondly, there may be effective co-ordination of effort on the part of agencies functioning in the same regional area or community, so that the various agencies may serve each area through a common pool of activities.

Training for Social Work

The contribution which social services make will depend to a considerable extent upon personnel and leadership. A general understanding of the philosophy and history of social work, the structure and functions of society, the nature and extent of social problems, the methods and techniques of social work, and of the details of the programmes and how best their results may be assessed, will help improve the quality and efficacy of all services organised by State and private agencies. The training of social workers should of course include knowledge of conditions prevailing in fields in which they are to work, and social workers must possess the spirit of service and the character and energy to execute programmes despite handicaps and limitations and with such resources as may be readily available.

There are several schools of social work in India and the setting up of some other institutions on similar lines is being contemplated in some of the States. There are important problems involved in these institutions which require specially qualified and experienced personnel, careful selection of candidates for training., special training for fields in which there is scope for employment, and adequate opportunities for field-work experience.

Trained social workers are needed in large numbers for rural areas. It should be possible for the existing schools of social work to draw students from rural areas and to arrange for their training in the field in selected centres organised by rural welfare agencies. Universities and colleges in or near rural areas could also develop training programmes for rural welfare. Agricultural colleges, could introduce intensive social welfare courses and field-work programmes as part of their curricula. Similar institutions with greater emphasis on social anthropology could be created in tribal, areas.

It is not possible for many voluntary organisations in the country to employ highly trained personnel for their ordinary programmes and activities. It is, therefore, necessary to arrange for training at the community level for field workers, instructors and supervisors. The existing schools of social work, specialised social service agencies, social welfare agencies functioning at the national and State level should provide opportunities for such training.

Arrangements for 'in-service' training should also be made by the larger voluntary organisations; which have worked in the field of social welfare for many years. Further, arrangements have to be made for the training of voluntary workers who will be needed in large numbers during the coming years. It is especially desirable that voluntary administrative and field personnel should be given some elementary training in social work.

The emergence of State social services and of large central organisations to deal with important social problems and the lack opportunities for higher training in the social sciences within the country indicate the need in selected cases for training and study abroad in specialised fields. It is necessary that persons who go abroad for training should first have sufficient knowledge and experience of Indian conditions and problems.

Research on Social Problems

Scientific research into social problems and fields of social work is at present limited to a few universities and the schools of social work. A provision of Rs. 50 lakhs has been made in the plan for research and investigations relating to social, economic and administrative problems of national development. Research studies now undertaken are not adequate or extensive enough for the purpose of getting a comprehensive knowledge of basic social problems. It is necessary to stress the need for ensuring that research personnel receive adequate training in methods and techniques. Secondly, it is important that the results of any research that is carried out should be made available to the public. The appropriate machinery for guiding research in the fields mentioned above is at present under consideration.

In the field of social research, it will be necessary to give a broad direction concerning the subjects on which research should be undertaken, carry out some important research projects, directly co-ordinate the work of research agencies in so far as this may be necessary, and assist these agencies in improving the quality of their work and bringing the results of research to the attention of the public. Universities, schools of social work, social welfare agencies and special research organisations can co-operate in research projects and in field investigations which could be of practical value in dealing with social problems. Assistance could also be given by way of literature and equipment needed for field research.

Resources Required by Social Service Agencies

The total resources of the country being limited, it is essential to nsure that funds available for social welfare programmes on the part of State agencies as well as voluntary organisations are put to the best possible use. This is a problem to which the proposed social welfare board could give detailed attention. While State may assist suitable voluntary agencies, the principle of self-help should be applied to social welfare, and the resources needed should, as far as possible, be obtained from the local communities. Social services are organised to carry out specific welfare activities. The total resources required by social service agencies in the country are obtained from State grants, income from endowments, public collections and income from special activities and from membership fees. Due to the prevailing economic conditions in the country, it is sometimes true that the public response is not as effective as it should be if the various organisations were to carry out their programmes efficiently. The appeal to the public is likely to yield greater results if care is taken to observe some elementary conditions such as the following:-

(1) the right methods for collection of funds are adopted,

(1) definite programmes of activities stating the manner in which funds are to be utilised by an agency are placed before the public., together with a psychological appeal,

(3) the effort of collection is well-organised,

(4) the appeal is addressed to as wide a section of the community as possible. Full use should be made of various modes of publicity and the public should feel that the cause is one worth supporting, and

(5) correct reports and accounts are provided and the public convinced of the integrity and the bona-fides of the organisations and the organisers concerned.

Funds available with endowments and trusts may be an important method of supplementing resources which the State and private agencies can provide. We, therefore, recommend enquiries by States into this subject which may offer a basis for legislation concerning the use for approved purposes of funds held by endowments and trusts.

Social Legislation

One of the important methods of bringing about progressive social change is social legislation. A good deal of legislation of basic importance has been enacted during recent years. The existing legislation needs to be scrutinised more intensively, especially with a view to finding out to what extent it serves the present social and economic objectives of the nation and to ascertain how far it can deal adequately with current social problems. Some machinery is needed for reviewing existing legislation and suggesting possible modifications, and if necessary, the repeal of obsolete laws in order that all existing legislation may be brought into conformity with the requirements of the Constitution. Social legislation has at times to be punitive in order to protect society from anti-social elements; but wherever possible, the legislation should be preventive and protective, and where it deals with the offender, its approach should be to rehabilitate the individual after eradicating the contributory factors to anti-social conduct.

Social legislation cannot by itself deal with social problems in an effective manner unless it is backed by the force of public opinion. Social legislation has also suffered owing to incomplete enforcement. This is especially due to lack of adequate machinery for enforcement, and also because of insufficient resources and personnel both with public and private agencies. Social legislation can be better enforced by associating social service agencies with agencies set up by the State. As regional communities become organised for social action, voluntary co-operation of the community based on enlightened understanding will go a long way in facilitating the enforcement of the law.

A critical survey of the prevailing legislation will suggest how far the legislative provisions are inadequate, to what extent enforcement must be strengthened and the directions in which new legislation is needed. The proposed social welfare board or social research organisation, or any other appropriate agency may undertake a comprehensive- survey to study the problem of social legislation. Legislation relating to the prevention of child marriages and the prevention of immoral traffic, certain housing and public health laws, laws affecting tribal areas and communities as also certain criminal laws constitute examples of social legislation which needs to be revised in the light of the existing needs and conditions. Among the laws which have to be enforced more effectively than they are at present are those relating to offences on the part of children, prevention of beggary and the control of prostitution. New legislation is required for the effective operation of social services in various fields. The registration of social service agencies with a view to inspection and sanction of grants-in-aid is one of the primary needs.

WOMEN'S WELFARE

In order that the woman may be allowed to fulfil her legitimate role in the family and the community, adequate services need to be promoted for her welfare. The position and functions of the woman differ to a great extent in different communities, and, therefore, community welfare agencies will have to workout their programmes and activities according to the specific requirments of the areas in which they work.

Important problems relating to the status and rights of woman have to be dealt with by legislation. Special organisations on the part of the Central or State Governments for promoting the welfare of women have not yet been developed to any great extent. Well-organised social service departments are needed in the States if they are to initiate more comprehensive programmes of woman and child welfare and achieve better co-ordination between the efforts of public and private agencies.

The major burden of organising activities for the benefit of the vast female population has to be borne by private agencies which have already done considerable work for the promotion of women's welfare. The All-

India Women's Conference has 37 branches and about 300 'sub-branches' in the country. The National Council of Women in India has 12 major branches, and the Girl Guides Association, the National Y.W.C.A., the Association for Moral and Social Hygiene, and the Trained Nurses Association in India, are affiliated to it. The Kasturba Gandhi National Memorial Trust does extensive work for the welfare of women and children in rural areas and has representatives to carry out activities in eighteen States. There are numerous small organisations all over the country which have done valuable work for women. These organisations provide dispensaries and maternity centres, homes for destitute children and shelter homes for women. They also organise programmes for education, recreation and training in-handicrafts.

Organised efforts are needed to stimulate activities at the community level, both in rural and urban areas. This should be done by community centres, social education agencies, and agencies working for the welfare of under-employed groups, by organising groups of women who could come together for activities such as recreation, education, arts and crafts, and co-operative participation in social and economic activities of the whole country. Groups could also be organised as " mothers' clubs or unions " in all ante-natal and post-natal clinics, milk centres, co-operatives, and as a part of trade union activities. Such groups could especially be organised in slum areas and backward areas and amongst working women and women of backward classes in general. A large number of voluntary workers will be required for such groups, and these could be recruited by women's welfare organisations. Girl guides and girl students in high schools and universities could assist in these activities as part of, a programme organised on a national basis. The existing women's organisations in the country could be strengthened if their membership and activities are extended, and if they organise programmes for creating women's organisations in towns and in the larger villages. Such local organisations need trained workers, guidance and assistance which could be given by leading women's organisations through travelling workers, training camps, instructional manuals, and other literature.

For various reasons the available statistics on commercial vice are limited and unreliable. India is a signatory to the international agreement for the suppression of traffic in persons and of prostitution which was reached in 1950. However, clandestine prostitution and even brothels continue to- exist in the country together with tolerated areas in some of the cities.

Clandestine prostitution exists in many forms and the danger of the evil is augmented when the woman is not assured economic security by the family or the community, or when she is psychologically maladjusted in terms of her sexual and material desires, or when her economic activities do not permit a normal family life. This kind of prostitution is further promoted by activities of persons who organise traffic in women and children. Immoral trafficking sometimes takes place as between backward and poor rural areas on the one hand, and the more prosperous urban areas on the other. Inter-provincial trafficking is also not unknown.

Certain social evils are products of inherent maladjustments in the social order and their complete eradication needs basic social adjustments. It is realised that such adjustments are only possible when social justice is more effective, there are reduced opportunities for concentration of wealth, exploitation is eradicated, economic conditions are improved, and social morality is established by well- adjusted patterns of common behaviour at the basic community level. The following measures are suggested for dealing with the problem:

(1) an advisory committee should be set up by the Central Government to make proposals and review progress in respect of law and policy in different States relating to the prevention and treatment of social vice;

(2) enforcement of the law should be more effectively carried out; measures to enforce the law may include, wherever necessary, the creation of a separate vigilance branch within the police force;

(3) whenever it is found difficult to eradicate the tolerated areas, adequate arrangements should be made for medical assistance and facilities for the treatment of venereal diseases;

(4) wherever it is found that clandestine prostitution is in existence, efforts should be made to eradicate soliciting;

(5) institutions for the protection, care, shelter and rehabilitation of fallen women do not exist in sufficient number, and cases of neglect are frequent. There is a need for more institutions organised by local self-governing bodies and private social service agencies and provision for regulation, inspection and control of homes which should be under the management of trained personnel.

(6) there is a need to strengthen existing specialised and private agencies like the vigilance associations and societies for the preventions of traffic in women.

Child Welfare

The child, being always dependent, has to be provided for by its parents and the family, the community and-the State. Considering the size of the-population involved and the nature and complexity of the problem, the total responsibility of welfare has to be borne cumulatively by the family, the regional community, and the State at three different levels.

In a country where poverty is extensive, there is need to supplement the diet of children. Effective ways have to be devised by the State and private agencies to see that the necessary nourishment is received at least by under-nourished children in schools and in established institutions. To augment State resources, an effort should be made by each local community to assist educational institutions and child welfare organisations in supplementing the diet of the child in some way. At present, skimmed milk powder, cases of baby foods, semolina, vitamin tablets, pabulum cereals, codliver oil, etc., are received as gifts from various sources.

Efforts to organise collections in kind at the community level could be supplemented by grants-in-aid from charity trusts and local self-governing bodies. It is desirable that State organisations, the Red Cross, the Indian Council of Child Welfare and other important national and State organisations for child welfare should co-ordinate their efforts both for the collection and distribution of supplementary foods for children. The five most suitable agencies for the distribution of free foods to children at the community level are (1) milk centres (2) maternity and child welfare centres (3) community centres (4) day nurseries and schools, and (5) play centres.

The attention of the educational authorities is naturally concentrated in the early stages on formal education. The problem of feeblemindedness is gradually beginning to receive the attention of psychologists and educationists in the country. Uptil now there are no adequate institutions in the country for the care and treatment of feeble-minded children. A beginning has been made in dealing with this problem by the Society for the care, treatment, and training of children in need of special care. A few pilot projects in selected areas could be developed by specialised agencies for child welfare. One of the major handicaps in this respect is the absence of a sufficient number of trained psychologists and psychiatrists and teachers specially trained to (teal with mentally backward children. Provision should be made for training personnel as early as possible.

Child Guidance Clinics

The first child guidance clinic was organised in India in 1936. Since then a small number of child guidance clinics have been brought into existence in some of the larger cities. It is desirable that at least one child guidance clinic should be brought into existence in every State and, wherever possible, such clinics should be organised by municipalities. The Organisation of this important service is also likely to be handicapped due to want of psychiatrists and child psychologists. It is essential to train a number of psychologists and case, workers in the schools of social work in order to provide trained personnel for dealing with problem children.

Greches

An important service which has already made considerable headway in India for the welfare of children is the Organisation of creches, day nurseries and other types of pre-schools. In large factories in major cities, already a number of creches are organised with a reasonable standard of efficiency in the interest for children whose mothers work in the factories. In 1951, Bombay had 177 creches with about 3,000 children, Madras had 93 with about 2,334 children, Bihar had 26 with 796 children, Madhya Pradesh had 16 with 360 children and Uttar Pradesh had 7 with 126 children. These figures reveal that only a very small percentage of children of working mothers take advantage of these creches, specially because it is the tradition in India for children to be looked after by other women members of the family. As it is now compulsory under the Factories Act of 1948 to provide a creche in factories employing 250 or more women special efforts may be made by factory owners to induce mothers to send their children to the creches.

Play is a vital need in the life of the child; and its playlife in the home, school and community environments consists of playthings, companionship, and playground activities. Local self-governing bodies as well as the community should provide playspace for children either as a reserved part of a community playground, or as a separate playground equipped with suitable accessories for play. Only a small number of fairly well-equipped playgrounds are in existence in the country; and their number needs to be very considerably increased in urban as well as rural areas. Proper maintenance and management of playgrounds are essential in order to provide necessary guidance, supervision, and protection to children during play hours. Such a playground service could be provided by voluntary welfare agencies and youth and students' organisations.

Childcare Centres

In order to extend the scope of children's recreations, the programmes for children's centres are now being expanded so that they can be equipped with playgrounds, indoor space for a children's library, a dramatic hall, and facilities for developing child arts and handicrafts. Such centres may also provide a case work service where it is not possible to organise a child guidance clinic.

One of the most difficult problems which deserves urgent consideration is the problem of lone, orphaned, neglected, deserted and destitute children. It is necessary to develop special institutions, children's villages, boys' towns and similar organisations where a large number of such children could be given protection, shelter, care, education and training till they are rehabilitated and can function in a normal way. At present, such institutions are mainly organised by private agencies, and especially by children's aid societies. Most of these institutions deal with a very small number of children, and it is desirable to initiate a number of pilot projects where a large number of children could be brought together under the care of specialised social welfare agencies in the various States.

The practice of adoption has existed in India for centuries. Such religious adoptions are not legally controlled. Besides, this benefit is invariably given to the boy. In some cases the orphaned child is institutionalised, or becomes a beggar, or becomes a victim of illegal trafficking and exploitation. Orphanages exist all over the country, both in urban and rural areas. The need to ensure registration, supervision and control of these institutions is now realised, and legislation and machinery of enforcement have to be devised to protect children in institutions organised by private agencies. Such institutions, with the support of the Government, should be able to provide a reasonable opportunity for growth, development and rehabilitation of all the inmates.

Problem of Delinquency

The complexities of the problem of delinquency and the inadequacy of resources, institutions, and personnel have come in the way of a study of the nature and extent of the problem. At present, only a small number of delinquent children are dealt with, and the treatment given to them does not provide for full rehabilitation. The problem of delinquency is extensive because of the prevailing general conditions in which children are brought up. Poverty, neglect, slum life and frustration may lead to acts of delinquency. Case treatment often reveals the delinquency of the parent, experience of cruelty at home, and encouragement of delinquent acts by elders.

In some States progressive legislation for dealing with delinquency already exists in others, no legislation has yet been enacted. The Ministry of Education has drafted model legislation for the guidance of States. Most of the Children's Acts deal with neglected, dependent and destitute children, difficult, uncontrollable and delinquent children and victimised and exploited children. In some cases the provisions of the Children's Act are in conflict with Wards and Guardians Acts. All existing legislation and treatment should be reviewed from the standpoint of a more comprehensive approach towards the problem.

The weakest link in the treatment of the problem is the absence of one suitable agency for the enforcement of the legislation, the absence of an adequate police force, and inadequacy of court facilities, children's institutions, and probation officers. It is necessary to set up juvenile aid committees in cities, consisting of a small number of selected and specially trained police officials who will examine cases of delinquents, and deal with cases of minor delinquencies without reference to courts.

The inadequacy of existing certified schools' and fit-persons institutions is well known, and in order to provide the right conditions, a beginning has been made in some States to create children's villages, boys' towns and other institutions with proper conditions of rehabilitation. Pilot projects for this purpose are contemplated in certain States where the incidence of delinquency is high. Institutions like juvenile reformatories exist in the country, and these need to be adapted and re- organised to suit the present objectives. The practice of providing even temporary habitation and shelter to juveniles in correctional institutions where adult under-trials and prisoners live should be discontinued.

The general improvement of child welfare services in India requires greater coordination and better leadership for the several hundred child welfare organisations that exist in India. The child welfare movement, under the guidance of the Indian Council for Child Welfare needs to be encouraged and strengthened; and it should be made more representative of children's organisations in the country.

There should be a strong national headquarters to carry out the objectives of the movement, and maintain and improve standards of child welfare. It is proposed to create a national centre of child welfare in a central place, with similar organisations in some of the States. The national centre will become the experimental station, training centre, seat of pilot projects and clearing house for information and material on child welfare.

Though comparatively small in size, organisations for children have come into existence in different parts of India for providing recreation for children. The Balkan-ji-Bari is a developing Organisation and its main value lies in bringing together children from all over India in camps and national festivals. The Bachon-ki-Biradari and Kishore Dal are similar organisations in the north. Such organisations deserve the support of local self-governing bodies and child welfare agencies. The junior sections of the Boy Scouts and Girl Guides organisations have been long engaged in giving valuable training to children outside the educational institutions. These organisations help to develop children for a fitting role in the youth movement.

Family Welfare

There are a few agencies dealing exclusively with the problems of the family in India, and they cater mainly to local needs. Sectional groups assist their members with small doles and provide help in education, medical assistance and housing accommodation.

Recently, some family welfare agencies have come into existence in Madras, Bombay and other places. The case work method is being used to assist families in rural as well as urban slum areas. This is a small beginning which shows a new approach to family problems. The organisations of extensive community welfare programmes in urban and rural areas creates the possibility of organising family welfare services on a small scale, including especially a family counselling service. As more case workers become trained in the various schools of social work, it will be possible to undertake a survey of family maladjustments and handicaps in selected community areas and to assist families in dealing with their economic and pathological problems.

The programme of social education ought to' make a valuable contribution towards the promotion of family welfare. There is need to give general information to adults about subjects like family relationships, family planning, marital hygiene, domestic economy, mothercraft and homecraft. This information could be supplemented by a programme of audiovisual aids dealing with all aspects of family life. Family welfare agencies should be able to publish literature giving specific information about the treatment of family problems.

The Central as well as State Governments may assist private organisations, trusts and funds in creating and running institutions or centres for the development of small-scale industries, crafts and handicrafts. Such institutions will provide avenues of employment and training and help families in avoidng destitution or in supplementing small family incomes.

YOUTH WELFARE

Youth is the stage in life when, through training and development, immaturity approaches maturity for work, marriage, social participation and cultural attainment. The period of youth should stand for growth, development, preparation, action and leadership. Youth matures quickly in an atmosphere in which there is freedom, activity, recognition and opportunity. The life of youth should not be over-occupied with training and education, but there should be opportunity for self-expression, comradeship, community life, and national service.

The youth movement includes two kinds of organisations, namely, those which work for the welfare of youth, and those composed of the youth themselves. In varying degrees, youth organisations are interested in or are influenced by political emphasis. In order that youth organisations should grow and make an effective and continuing contribution to national life, their endeavour should be to give their main attention to activities which would promote youth welfare. Besides, the strength of the national youth movement can only be built up as a result of unity in action and comradeship amongst those who work for youth welfare in any of its aspects.

The objectives of the youth movement may be classified to cover two separate aspects of the movement: (1) those that contribute towards self-preparation, personality development, character formation and citizenship; and (2) those that lead to organised action in the service of the community and the nation.

Youth has with courage opposed conventionalism and unhelpful traditions, but the immediate task before youth in India is to organise and work hard to carry out constructive tasks in the national programme. There is need to coordinate the work of all youth organisations; into a single powerful youth movement, functioning through a national council of affiliated youth organisations. Such an Organisation, whilst permitting its members to work for their own objectives and carry out their programme independently, will work to build up the individual and collective strength of all youth organisations.

The national youth movement has to create a national headquarters with young men and women of vision and ability who should be trained youth organisers, aware of the prob- lems of youth, and trained to develop group work, recreational activities and national service programmes which can be quickly canalised into various fields of service. Assistance may be given by the State to the existing youth and other organisations to create and strengthen the youth movement.

Special measures are needed to strengthen the scout movement. The Bharat Scouts and Guides Organisation had 1,73,902 cubs, 2,65,296 scouts and about 50,000 bulbuls and guides on its rolls in 1951. The movement has 21,393 trained and warranted scouters and 3,997 helpers. The scout movement has to play a vital role in serving the younger generation and in organising them for the active service of the country. Not only has the movement to be extended to villages, but the quality of its service has to be developed. For this purpose the national as well as State headquarters have to be strengthened and adequately equipped for creating and training a larger number of scouters and promote efficient guidance and supervision to its units. The scout movement should receive the support of the States, the local self-governing bodies as well as the community. There should also be co-ordination of activities between the scout movement and the other youth and children's organisations.

The youth and student organisations should be able to provide an increasing number of scouters who will be required to extend the work of the movement in the near future. The National Cadet Corps is another movement for youth which functions in the universities for the promotion of physical fitness, discipline, character and the general fitness of youth for defence, national service and personal welfare. The membership of the National Cadet Corps is voluntary, but universities and educational authorities should encourage youth to take advantage of this Organisation, and membership of the National Cadet Corps should be considered an added qualification for the purpose of employment.

Youth needs guidance, advice and help with regard to personality problems, sex difficulties, and situations in home and community life. The Organisation of community centres in urban and rural areas will make " youth counselling " possible, provided there are mature persons who are given a brief training on youth problems, and who are willing to undertake counselling on a voluntary basis. It is possible to introduce " youth counselling " as one of the activities in educational institutions as well as in youth organisations and trade unions, and it could also form part of the labour welfare progress in factories.

Opportunity for physical activities, group companionship, arts, hobbies, and contact with Nature can be given through organised programmes of local boys' and girls' clubs, inventors' clubs, young farmers' clubs, hobby clubs, etc. These do not require large resources, and the younger folk themselves can contribute and find the necessary funds to run their own organisations as independent programmes or as part of community centres or as extra- curricular activities in educational institutions.

An important contribution towards the development of youth is made by youth camping and travelling programmes. A beginning has been made in India with a Youth Hostels Association, which is part of an international Organisation. The movement needs organisers, and houses with caretakers, which could be used as hostels. University hostels, dharamshalas, houses which can be spared, hutments on camp sites, and houses near holiday resorts should be made available to youth travellers with minimum equipment and boarding and lodging facilities at lowest cost.

The Government can help the youth movement by allowing special reduced rates on railways, steamships, and State and municipal motor services to members of approved youth organisations. Whenever merit awards are given to youth in universities, and sports, cultural and other organisations, it should be possible to give travel prizes and journey scholarships.

Youth and national service-Youth have made a vital contribution to the struggle for freedom, and they must be given the opportunity to give their contributions to constructive activities and programmes of economic development and social welfare. Youth participation in constructive activities should be based on personal inclination and interests, and youth should be encouraged to become members of organisations that carry out specific activities amongst the people or there could be special youth groups for carrying out specific programmes. It is also possible for educational institutions to organise "service clubs" as one of the extra curricular activities. The enthusiastic participation of youth is required in programmes and activities for promoting physical fitness and community recreation, social education, child welfare and youth organisation. Youth could also render valuable help to institutes organised to render different types of service to the needy, handicapped and maladjusted members of society.

The subject of fitness deals with the maintenance and improvement of health of every citizen in order to develop efficiency. In the absence of legislation in the form of a National Fitness Act, it is necessary that physical fitness programmes are promoted by the States, as well as by the community.

It is possible for a nation to attain by organised effort and education certain physical qualities, abilities and skills so as to be able to perform the normal functions of life, be prepared for the protection of home and nation in times of external agression and danger, and contribute towards national efficiency for economic production. A physical fitness standard for the individual should include the three factors of agility, strength and endurance which are the basis of all physical qualities and skills. In order to achieve the above, a national standard of physical achievement for all adults has to be laid down.

In a country like India, with numerous climatic, regional and racial differences, a universally applicable national standard may be difficult to attain and allowance will have to be made for sex differences, the racial factor, types of physical region, climatic conditions, standard and content of nutrition, and prevailing averages of height and weight for specific racial groups. The standards to be achieved may be laid down by a committee of health and education experts and other social scientists after consulting authorities and ascertaining conditions in different parts of the country. It is possible for every individual to strive to attain this standard individually; but the State, educational authorities and. private social welfare and especially physical welfare agencies should attempt to provide facilities and opportunities to assist the individual to attain this standard. The community project authorities, the Bharat Sewak Samaj, all sports and play-ground organisations and universities should aim at reaching the proposed national standards.

The maintenance and promotion of national physical fitness requires the proper management of housing and sanitation, the care of diet, the need for relaxation and rest, the promotion of play-ground, sports, physical culture and camping movements, execution of intensive programmes of child welfare, the protection of the health of working men and women, and the adoption of preventive measures against diseases and psychological disorders like neurosis.

Play-ground programmes are naturally spread over in different areas. Regional co-ordination of all agencies and activities will promote the growth of leadership, the training of personnel and the development as well as the economic use of resources. National organisations for physical education, sports, recreations, etc., should be strengthened, so that they can guide and assist the building up of play-ground activities, athletics, community recreation and yogic exercises. As play-ground activities are to be developed through community programmes, and as youth activities are also to be promoted extensively, there will be increasing demand for leadership in these fields. It is suggested that one of the existing training institutes for physical education should be converted into a national institute.

As national fitness programmes involve activities for large numbers of persons, the problem of resources becomes the greatest handicap in the promotion of the movement. It is imperative that some kind of playground should be available for the use of every community centre, school and youth Organisation. Equipment is also needed for physical fitness programmes. When developing play-ground programmes, it is necessary to keep in view the four important objectives of recreation, education, leadership training, and social participation. India has yet to make much headway in the field of sports and steady support and encouragement are needed.

India has a rich gamelore with a variety of games adapted to age and sex groups and to local physical conditions and cultural patterns. There is need to survey play activities in different areas, prepare a manual of instructions for specially selected games, and enrich the gamelore of the whole country by organised publicity through documentary films demonstrating each game. Indian gymnastic programmes have considerable appeal in urban as well as rural areas. Community programmes should help the revival and extension of such activities in every part of the country.

Crime and Correctional Administration

Research in the problem of crime in India has not yet made sufficient advance. The immediate task is to change or modify existing policies and programmes in order to adjust them to new objectives which seek to protect the interest of society and achieve a total rehabilitation of the offender. Crime is stimulated by conditions prevailing in society and it is due to personal and psychological factors. Economic conditions have always been a factor contributing to crime. Intensive surveys to study the causes, nature and extent of crime should be undertaken by research organisations, universities and other private agencies. The treatment of the crime, problem is intimately related to the nature of legislation, and the approach of the judiciary to crime. So far there has been no basic approach towards the various problems of correctional administration, but a number of useful steps have been recently taken by States and there is growing interest in the reform of penal administration.

The problem of correctional administration has to be dealt with in three stages: the pre-committal stage; the administration of correctional institutions; and probation and after-care. The principle that no person should be considered an offender till he is proved guilty should govern the treatment of accused and under-trial persons. The administration of police lock-ups and jails needs to be reviewed in the interest of the proper treatment of the inmates of the lock-ups. Special care must be taken when first offenders are committed to jails, so that no serious psychological harm is done to them. The administration of correctional institutions is governed by jail manuals. A recent conference of State Inspectors-General of Prisons has proposed the appointment of a committee to suggest the basis on which jail manuals may be revised to suit the new objectives, methods and programmes of correctional institutions, remove the inflexibility of rules, and permit greater freedom to the authorities on the spot to interpret sympathetically the rules so as to serve the objects of rehabilitation. Changes in the jail manuals will naturally require a revision of the Prison and Prisoners' Act which would need to be modified to meet changes in correctional administration.

The need to utilise prisons as agencies for the rehabilitation of prisoners is generally accepted. Modern principles of penology require that each prisoner is to be dealt with as an individual, and corrective handling should be so devised as to be in consonance with his abilities, aptitudes, back-ground and also with the paramount purpose of enabling him to earn his living honestly as a law-abiding member of society. While this must be the ideal and all plans must be directed to this end, the possibility of utilising the manpower resources represented by prisoners on projects of socially constructive character should be fully explored. Central prisons and district jails should receive the assistance of Departments such as those concerned with industries, agriculture and irrigation, so that the maximum advantage can be taken of the labour available in correctional institutions.

A probation and after-care service is likely to minimise the cost of maintenance, as prisoners will not be called upon to serve long sentences during which they will be maintained by State Governments. As life in prison has to be organised so that the inmates live as a community and as the method of case work is to be increasingly used to deal with individual cases in correctional institutions, welfare officers should be progressively employed in central prisons and first grade district jails. Officials of correctional institutions should be given special training both before employment and during service.

Prisons and jails may need to be reconditioned so as to provide arrangements to suit different classes of prisoners. Separate correctional institutions may be provided for female convicts. It should also be possible to develop open and close farm workshop prisons, agricultural colonies, and work camps at important work projects. The provision for Borstals, both open and closed, will also need to be expanded. It will be necessary to bring about greater uniformity in legislation applicable to first offenders and others charged more than once for minor offences. The appointment of probation officers and the release of prisoners on parole should remove a great deal of congestion from correctional institutions, reduce the cost of prison administration, and enable many prisoners to live as normal citizens after they have served their sentences.

The work of private agencies like prisoners' aid societies and district probation and after-care associations has suffered on account of limited resources. It is desirable to entrust after-care work to probation officers, and a beginning may be made by organising after- care departments in central prisons and first grade district jails to deal with problems relating to work and employment, housing, health and family relationship.

New developments in the administration and programmes of correctional institutions require the guidance and advice of experienced personnel working together in a central organisation. Such an organisation can assist programmes in the States, undertake experimental work and pilot projects, and function as a centre of information and publicity on all matters relating to correctional administration. Recognising the need for such a central organisation, the recent conference of Inspectors-General of Prisons recommended that a national bureau of correctional institutions may be established in the Ministry of Home Affairs.

Welfare of Handicapped Persons

The physically handicapped person, if he is not able to receive medical attention, or when such attention is found to be of no avail, has to depend upon his family for maintenance and shelter. Absence of family support leads to beggary, or dependence upon public charity. Inadequate medical treatment, absence of vocational training, and lack of opportunities for social adjustment of the persons to the environment has contributed to the sufferings of a large number of persons who ought to receive the intelligent assistance of the community, and if possible an effective assistance from the State. Physically handicapped persons are classified as

(1) those lacking in one or more physical senses, i.e., blindness and deafness, or combinations;

(2) those suffering from movement difficulties; i.e., orthopedic, malnutrities and cardiacs; and

(3) lepers, epileptics, rachitics, and dumb persons.

The total number of afflicted persons in India has hardly ever been correctly estimated. This is due to defective enumeration, lack of definitions, and the desire of persons to avoid publicity to their handicaps. To obtain better estimates of afflicted persons, sample surveys in selected urban and rural areas are needed. Some provision for physically handicapped persons exists in several States. Voluntary associations which are already working the welfare programmes for this class of persons need to be encouraged and assisted.

3

Working for the Welfare of Urban Children

Around a billion children live in urban areas-close to half the world's children. They live in sprawling mega-cities and in provincial towns, in cities that have existed for centuries and in rapidly growing centres within areas still perceived as predominantly rural. Most of the world's urban children – over 80 per cent of them – live in Africa, Asia and Latin America, and their numbers are growing fast. Africa, one of the least urbanised regions, already has more than twice as many urban children as North America.

Urban children are generally considered to be better off than rural children: healthier, better housed, better educated and with access to a wider range of services and opportunities. Cities can indeed offer these advantages, but the reality is that hundreds of millions of urban children live in deep poverty, their rights neglected, their needs unmet, their prospects damaged by conditions that threaten their health and undermine their development.

There are at least two reasons why urban children should be expected to enjoy greater opportunities than rural children as regards survival and development. The first is that urban areas provide significant economies of scale and proximity for the delivery of health care and education, piped water and emergency services and the provision for good quality sanitation and drainage. The second is that many cities have a more prosperous economic base than rural areas, providing higher average incomes for large sections of the population and greater possibilities for governments or private utilities to fund basic services.

Making use of this potential 'urban advantage' depends on structures of competent, effective local governance in cities and smaller urban areas. The application of the principles of good governance – including accountability, equity and social inclusion – at the local level, with the full and committed involvement of municipal government structures, is a prime opportunity to promote and act upon a commitment to children's rights. This commitment can be translated into all aspects of urban life, from planning, policy making and budgetary decisions, to service provision and the introduction of participatory structures.

In the absence of 'good governance' – and with the lack of investment in infrastructure, basic social services and waste management that this absence implies – an urban concentration of children and their families becomes a serious disadvantage. As the World Health Organisation has recognised, when infrastructure and services are lacking, urban settlements are among the world's most life-threatening environments.

Many low income countries still have urban child mortality rates as high as 100 to 200 per 1000 live births. In Africa, for example, some of the highest urban mortality rates for children include Chad, Madagascar, Mozambique, and Zambia. Moreover, high as these aggregate figures are, they mask even higher levels in poor urban districts. Figures from India, where 24 per cent of the total urban population of 285 million are classified as poor,indicate that more than half of the country's poor urban children are underweight and/or stunted; a high proportion are severely undernourished – 23 per cent in weight-for-age and 30 per cent in height-for-age. 50 per cent of poor urban children are only partially vaccinated, and another 18 per cent are not vaccinated at all. More than 80 per cent of poor children in India's urban areas have anaemia.

A final compelling reason for considering the situation of urban children lies in the fact that, despite the long term trend towards more urbanised societies, many governments in Africa, Asia and Latin America still lack a fully developed urban policy, despite there being substantial differences between most rural and urban areas as regards the factors that pose the greatest threats to child survival, protection and development. Clearly, effective programmes for poor and excluded children depend on an understanding of these differences.

Good Governance and Promotion of Child Rights

In any context, urban or rural, good governance and the full enjoyment of human rights are mutually reinforcing: human rights inform the principles of good governance and, in turn, a key characteristic of good governance is the promotion of these rights. The world's urban settlements provide particularly fertile ground for the establishment and development of systems of good local governance guided by human rights principles and, in particular, for the application of the general principles and other provisions of the 1989 Convention on the Rights of the Child (CRC). While all provisions of the CRC apply to all children in every situation, some articles are particularly salient in the urban context:

— *Article 16*: No child shall be subjected to arbitrary or unlawful interference with his or her privacy, family, home or correspondence ... .

- *Article 18*: States Parties shall render appropriate assistance to parents and legal guardians in the performance of their child-rearing responsibilities ... shall ensure the development of institutions, facilities and services for the care of children. ... shall take all appropriate measures to ensure that children of working parents have the right to benefit from child-care services and facilities for which they are eligible.
- *Article 24*: States Parties recognise the right of the child to the enjoyment of the highest attainable standard of health and to facilities for the treatment of illness and rehabilitation of health. States Parties shall strive to ensure that no child is deprived of his or her right of access to such health care services. ... shall take appropriate measures: (a) To diminish infant and child mortality; (b) To ensure the provision of necessary medical assistance and health care to all children with emphasis on the development of primary health care; (c) To combat disease and malnutrition ... through the provision of adequate nutritious foods and clean drinking water, taking into consideration the dangers and risks of environmental pollution;
- *Article 27*: States Parties recognise the right of every child to a standard of living adequate for the child's physical, mental, spiritual, moral and social development. States Parties, in accordance with national conditions and within their means, shall take appropriate measures to assist parents and others responsible for the child to implement this right and shall in case of need provide material assistance and support programmes, particularly with regard to nutrition, clothing and housing.
- *Article 28*: States Parties recognise the right of the child to education, and they shall, in particular: (a)

Make primary education compulsory and available free to all; ... (e) Take measures to encourage regular attendance at schools and the reduction of drop-out rates.

- *Article 31*: States Parties recognise the right of the child to rest and leisure, to engage in play and recreational activities appropriate to the age of the child and to participate freely in cultural life and the arts.
- *Article 32*: States Parties recognise the right of the child to be protected from economic exploitation and from performing any work that is likely to be hasardous or to interfere with the child's education, or to be harmful to the child's health or physical, mental, spiritual, moral or social development.

The explicit right of every child to enjoy adequate living conditions, a safe environment and access to housing and basic social services, including education and health, is also underlined in other human rights standards. Article 25 of the 1948 Universal Declaration of Human Rights states that "everyone has the right to a standard of living adequate for the health and well-being of himself and his family, including food, clothing, housing and medical care and necessary social services ... . ". These or similar principles are included in other important instruments:

- Article 21 of the 1951 International Convention Relating to the Status of Refugees;
- Principle 2 of the 1961 International Labour Organisation Recommendation No. 115, on Worker's Housing;
- Article 5 of the 1965 International Convention on the Elimination of all Forms of Racial Discrimination;
- Article 11 of the 1966 International Covenant on Economic, Social and Cultural Rights;

— Article 43 of the 1990 International Convention on the Protection of the Rights of All Migrant Workers and Members of Their Families.

Formal declarations from high level international encounters help to re-emphasize periodically the importance of promoting specific initiatives for urban dwellers including transparent and accountable governance, fair distribution of income, provision of health services and free education, adequate shelter and nutrition, promotion of employment opportunites, and a constant attention to the special needs of women and children.

Notable in this regard are the Declaration on Human Settlements adopted by the UN Conference on Human Settlement in 1976 in Vancouver, the Declaration on Social Development adopted at the 1995 World Summit for Social Development in Copenhagen, and the Declaration on Human Settlements adopted in 1996 by the UN Conference on Human Settlements in Istanbul. In addition, *A World Fit for Children*, the outcome document from the UN General Assembly Special Session on Children held in May 2002, emphasizes the role of local governments and authorities to strengthen partnerships at all levels and ensure that children are at the centre of agendas for development. The same document also draws attention to the importance of promoting national and sub-national policies for children, and to developing capacity – and particularly community capacity – for monitoring and assessment.

Trends of Urban Development

Today, most of the world's urban population is to be found in Asia, Latin America and Africa. Indeed, one quarter of the world's urban population lives in only two countries – China and India. Europe too has a sizeable share of the urban population – one fifth of the world's 3 billion urban dwellers. During the 20century, the world's urban population grew more than tenfold and the average size of the 100 largest cities increased more than eightfold. The proportion of people living in urban areas grew from less than 15 per cent in 1900 to an estimated 48 percent by 2002. This change has been fuelled by expansion in the world's economy, most of which has taken place in industrial and service enterprises located in urban areas. Since most economic growth continues to be in urban-based enterprises, the trend towards ever larger urban populations is likely to continue.

Where cities have demonstrated dramatic growth rates, this usually reflects a rapid expansion of economic activities. Such growth is frequently associated with very poor conditions – but growth, of itself, is rarely the reason for this. For example, the Brazilian city of Porto Alegre has been one of the world's fastest growing cities over the last 40 years, but nonetheless, citizens there have a life expectancy of 74 years compared to a national average of 67.

Rapid growth rates alone are therefore an inadequate explanation for poor conditions: cities such as Miami, Houston, Dallas and Phoenix all grew faster than most large African and Asian cities over the last century. Indeed, some of the worst conditions are to be found in cities around the world that have grown slowly or even declined in size.

Many of the largest and fastest growing cities in all regions are those that have been most successful in increasing their role within the globalising economy. Some of these cities, such as Dhaka and Bangkok, are their nation's capital and largest city. Others, such as Shenzen in China and Bangalore in India, are changing the urban geography of their nation as they grow to challenge older and larger cities.

Despite the growing influence of globalisation, local political and demographic contexts continue to shape the form that urbanisation takes. A significant part of the 'urban explosion' in many African nations around independence was simply women and children joining their husbands and fathers, once colonial restrictions had been removed. In addition, in many parts of Africa, urban change has also been profoundly influenced by civil wars and the sheer number of refugees seeking new bases for their livelihoods. HIV/AIDS has also had a significant impact on rural-urban population movements, as children who have lost their parents to this disease (and who may have been unable to inherit their parents' land because they do not have a birth certificate to prove their parentage) are drawn to urban centres in search of a livelihood.

Dramatic urban change in China since the late 1970s has been driven not only by rapid expansion in its economy, but also by the reduction in controls on rural to urban population movement. In much of Latin America, urban trends have been shaped by the introduction of, or return to, democratic rule, the shift from import substitution to export promotion, serious economic problems and, in many cases, decentralisation and stronger democracy at the level of local government.

The dissolving of the Soviet Union and its economic bloc and the breaking up or reshaping of several states in Europe has inevitably had an impact upon the urban systems and trends of these countries. Urban growth can also be influenced simply by rapid population growth rates. Thus, while broad economic changes remain the main influence on the proportion of the world's population living in urban areas, there are many other factors that influence the scale and nature of urban change within each nation or region.

Poverty ans Social Exclusion

Aggregate statistics almost inevitably indicate that urban populations are better off than national populations as a whole because middle and upper income groups tend to be concentrated in urban areas. This does not mean, however, that the whole population of 'privileged' cities benefits from this relative wealth. Where statistics are available for low-income districts, they often show infant or child mortality rates many times higher than the city average, and levels of provision for water and sanitation far below the average.

In low-income countries it is common for between a third and half of a nation's urban population, or that of a particular city, to have incomes below the official poverty line; and in many cases more than half. Proportions below poverty lines can be high even in wealthier nations – for instance, in 1990 Buenos Aires was one of the wealthiest cities in Latin America, but nevertheless, 34. 5 percent of the city's population were classified as poor.

The proportion is now much higher as a result of the economic crisis. But many of these official statistics still underestimate the gravity of the situation: they purport to measure the proportion of people 'living in poverty,' but exclude any criteria related to housing conditions, including access to water and sanitation.

Almost all official statistics use a poverty line based on estimates of the cost of food needed to meet nutritional requirements, with a small amount generally included for non-food essentials. This assumes that households are not poor when their income rises above this defined level. According to these definitions, a household with no secure home, no provision for water, sanitation and electricity, no access to health care, and no children in school would be considered as suffering the same deprivations as a household with the same income but with all these. This helps explain why estimates of the scale of urban poverty worldwide are so much lower than the estimates for the number of people living in very poor quality housing that lacks basic services.

Basing poverty lines primarily on the cost of food is especially problematic in cities, since a defining characteristic of cities is the commercialisation of the majority of goods and services. Most urban households face high costs for nonfood essentials including rent, water and sanitation, transport, keeping children in school, health care and medicines, fuel and child-care.

Many low-income households pay 20-30 per cent of their income on rent. A study of the small Russian town of Novocherkassk, with a population of some 190,000, found that while rent and utility charges represented only 5 per cent of the total expenditure of the richest tenth of the population, this figure was as high as 66 per cent for the poorest tenth. It is common for water, health care and transport each to take 5 or more per cent of income.

Many poor urban households pay particularly high prices for essentials. For instance, in illegal settlements, those who have to use water vendors or kiosks often pay many times more per litre than middle or upper income groups with piped water connections. In Bangkok, Thailand, for example, the price of water from a vendor can be up to five times higher than the price charged by the public utility; in Nouakchott, Mauritania, the price can be 10 times higher – and as much as 40 times higher when there is a water shortage; while in Karachi, Pakistan, the price from private vendors can be anything between 28 and 83 times higher than that of the public utility.

The fact that poverty lines in low and middle income countries make little or no allowance for the cost of housing and associated services is particularly puzzling, given that these costs are critical in influencing poverty levels in most high income countries. Moreover, official statistics can overstate access to urban services because the criteria upon which they are based can give a misleading impression of the standard and availability of facilities. For example, official surveys may classify urban residents living within 100 metres of a piped water supply as 'adequately served' even when there are 500 people to each tap and the supply is intermittent or lacking. They may classify households with 'access to a latrine' as adequately served even when this latrine is shared by many households and poorly maintained, or is a public toilet to which regular access is both difficult and costly. Of course, official statistics on service provision may overstate the extent and quality of provision in rural areas too.

Understanding the scale of the problem is complicated by the fact that countries use different criteria for setting urban poverty lines, thus limiting the validity of international comparisons. A low proportion living in poverty may simply reflect an unrealistic poverty line. Universal poverty lines are even more misleading, since they take no account of differences in the income needed to avoid poverty between and within countries.

Few official development statistics give specific attention to the poverty status of urban children. While the 1980s saw proven child survival gains for most countries, national indicators show limited progress in child well being from 1990 to 2000. Reductions in infant and child mortality rates slowed or stopped in many low and middle income nations; in African nations most affected by HIV/AIDS, civil conflict and declining economy, they rose sharply. The incidence of malnutrition declined far less during the 1990s than in the two previous decades, except in Latin America. In Africa and the Middle East the number of underweight children rose during the 1990s. There are few indicators of how these trends are played out in urban areas. In Latin America, child poverty rose in absolute terms and faster than overall poverty as worsening income distribution pushed up the number of working poor with dependent children.

Given that more than three quarters of the region's population live in urban areas, this would seem to imply that these areas have experienced a rise in the level of child poverty. In most high-income nations, the basis on which poverty is defined has changed from absolute to relative measures, with poverty lines set as a percentage of median income. Households with incomes below 40 or 50 per cent of the national median are defined as poor. In part, this reflects success in reducing absolute poverty. But even 'relative' poverty can mean hunger, poor health, dilapidated housing, inadequate schools, violent neighbourhoods, social exclusion and little opportunity.

Furthermore, some of the nations with the highest levels of child poverty, or the largest increases in poverty over the last two decades, are also nations where per capita income has increased substantially – notably the USA and the United Kingdom. Recent figures in the United Kingdom indicate that one out of three children is poor, that is, living below half the mean level of income on an 'after housing costs' basis, although the proportion is now falling.

In the USA, where poverty rates are highest in urban areas, over 30 per cent of urban children fall below poverty lines; the proportion of urban children considered to be at high risk has grown by 58 per cent since 1976. By contrast, several other high-income nations, including Belgium, Norway and Sweden, have less than 5 per cent of children living in poverty. This is largely due to social and economic policies in these countries that address inequalities.

Factors Contributing to Urban Poverty

The factors contributing to poverty among children and their families in urban areas exist at every level from the most local to the international. The immediate causes of deprivation are often more obvious and easily acted upon, but real change also requires action on the complex and wide-ranging causes that underpin this condition, including the lack of community empowerment and participation.

For example, initiatives to enrol poor urban children in school should address the factors that subsequently push many children to drop out of education and seek work. These include the economic situation of the child's family and the costs incurred by the child attending school; the facilities available to and the organisational capacity of local communities; the unequal distribution and quality of schools within urban areas; prevailing discrimination against certain groups, including girls, immigrants, minorities and children with disabilities; and the failure of governments, both local and national, to respond in practical terms to education as a basic human right.

No summary of the underlying and basic causes of child deprivation can do justice to all such factors. This Digest focuses on three key themes: the quality of local and national governance, growing inequality within nations, and the difficulties faced by many countries in developing a stable economic base.

Quality of Governance

Shifting attention to the causes that underpin poverty and exclusion among urban children requires a new focus on two of the most complex and politically controversial issues within nations – the distribution of power, authority and resources among different levels of government, and the quality of 'governance' in terms of its responsiveness, accountability, transparency and quality of engagement with civil society. Almost all policies, programmes and decisions by governments (and international agencies) have implications for urban children.

Urban areas, by their nature, are points of concentration for, and connection to, the monetary economy. The stability of urban households with children is tied to the underlying and basic causes of economic change in urban areas, and the well-being of urban children (as well as rural children) is tied to good economic performance nationally, and to fair distribution of the benefits of economic growth – through a commitment to pro-poor growth, stable incomes, unexploitative working practices, education and training programmes.

The size of inter-governmental transfers from central government to regional and local authorities is highly relevant for children because most responsibility for basic infrastructure and services lies with local government agencies, and most urban governments in Africa, Asia and Latin America lack the fiscal base to meet their multiple responsibilities for child health and development.

There are huge differentials between high and low income nations in the revenue per person controlled by local authorities (varying by factors of 100 or more), and even larger differentials in their capital investment capacity per person. In high income nations, the web of local institutions that serve, support and protect children (and parents) is taken for granted. Coverage for some services may be sub-standard, and some groups are illserved or excluded, but the vast majority of the urban population is served.

Inequality

Much child deprivation is linked to inequality within nations – including nations with good economic performance. According to available data, income inequality has increased in most nations, especially in Latin America and countries previously in the Soviet Bloc (which tend to be among the most urbanised of low and middle income nations).

Rising average urban incomes do not necessarily mean falling child poverty: in the United States child poverty rates have increased 31 per cent in urban areas and 50 per cent in suburban areas since the 1970s, despite the fact that real per capita incomes are much higher today than they were in 1970. Even falling unemployment may not mean a reduction in child deprivation: in the UK, the proportion of households with children with no income earner grew between 1985 and 1996, even though unemployment levels fell.

An analysis of child poverty in rich nations shows the importance of government policies and redistributive taxes as a means of reducing poverty levels or preventing them from rising too much during periods of economic difficulty; it indicates, too, that the withdrawal of state support for the unemployed or those on low income can increase child poverty even during periods of economic prosperity.

There is no evidence that measures to keep down child poverty have an adverse effect on economic growth. Many of the world's wealthiest nations also have the lowest levels of child poverty and the highest levels of inter-governmental transfer. It is worth noting the emphasis among many nations with the lowest levels of child poverty on getting the unemployed back to work. In many low and middle income nations, governments have been ineffective in establishing social policies that improve provision for children in general and that support the most vulnerable children.

The liberalising agenda has cut the resources available to governments, but without ensuring that the poorest and most vulnerable groups are not most affected. In China, for example, sweeping socio-economic reform is providing positive benefits to a large number of people. However some segments of society are being left behind. The disappearance of guaranteed housing, medical services, pensions and other basic services and the reform of the state-owned enterprise system are provoking new kinds of economic, social and psychological stress for disadvantaged families.

In this rapid development process, children, especially girls, become vulnerable to and, often, victims of neglect, abuse and exploitation. The serious impacts on children of the macro-economic reforms promoted by the World Bank and the IMF in the early 1980s came as a surprise to most of their proponents, who had assumed that the resulting economic growth would more than compensate for short term losses. Rarely was provision made to protect the social expenditures with most importance for child development. This is still the case in many nations. Public expenditure on health is very low and stagnating in low income nations and falling marginally in middle income nations.

Effects of Global Economy

The very poor economic performance of the world's low income nations and the economic deterioration in many middle income nations underlies much child deprivation. It also underpins the very large debt burdens that so many nations face. A globalising world economy creates winners and losers, and growing inequality between nations presents particular challenges for children.

Many nations have faced significant declines in per capita incomes in recent years. The situation in Eastern Europe, Central Asia and most of Sub-Saharan Africa during the 1990s has been particularly extreme. Sharp rises in unemployment, reductions in wages and, often, increases in the price of basic goods have had serious impacts upon large sections of the urban (and rural) population. In Tajikistan, for example, by 1996 real GDP had fallen to 40 per cent of its 1990 level, while government expenditure dropped from 65 per cent of GDP in 1992 to 16 per cent in 1998.

It is difficult to protect children from lower income households in the face of both falling incomes and declining government expenditures. Urban populations may be more vulnerable to these changes because of their dependence on the monetary economy for their livelihoods, but in most locations there are so many linkages between rural and urban areas that it is difficult to discuss these separately. For instance, in Accra, Ghana's largest city, the proportion of the population living in poverty increased rapidly between 1987 and 1993, whereas it decreased in both rural areas and other urban areas. But growing poverty in Accra may have serious impacts, including fewer job opportunities for rural dwellers, less remittance flows to rural areas, less urban demand for rural products, and more urban to rural migration, which in turn increases dependency burdens in rural areas. Strong rural-urban interactions and inter-depen-dencies mean that structural adjustment affects both rural and urban populations. When rural poverty grows, this generally brings serious impacts to many urban areas, especially those whose economies depend on demand from rural producers and consumers.

Urban Living Conditions

Urban areas present some very specific challenges for those in poverty, and these challenges, in turn, have significant and often disproportionate impacts on children and adolescents, undermining their rights and their well being in ways that require particular responses.

Infrastructure

Environmental conditions are generally particularly poor in low income urban districts. Wherever there are high concentrations of people and of waste, the potential for contamination, contagion and disease is great. When this potential is not countered by effective provision, health costs are very high and infants and young children are disproportionately affected.

Millions of urban infants and children die each year, and many more suffer from illnesses or injuries that can and should be prevented. Age-related risk factors include immature immune systems, higher exposure to pathogens, greater susceptibility to particular chemicals and inadequate understanding of how to avoid hazards.

In cities served by piped water, sanitation, drainage, waste removal and a good health care system, child mortality rates are generally around 10 per 1000 live births, and few deaths are the result of environmental hazards. In contrast, in cities or neighbourhoods with inadequate provision, it is common for child mortality rates to be 10 or 20 times this, and for environmental hazards to be major causes. And aggregate figures can disguise significant intra-urban variations; for example, surveys in seven settlements in Karachi found that infant mortality rates varied from 33 to as many as 209 per 1000 live births. Differentials are also evident in cities in high income nations, although mortality rates are much lower and are not as closely related to environmental factors. In

Glasgow, United Kingdom, in 1990, the infant mortality rate in a poor area was 47 per thousand live births, compared to 10 per thousand for a more affluent suburb. Similarly, in Washington DC in 1997, infant mortality rates, broken down by ward, show considerable variation – from a rate of 2. 8 per thousand in a high income area to a rate of 16 per thousand in one of the poorer wards.

The information base for a precise identification of the relative importance of different causes or risk factors is limited: there is a clear need for better data if the dynamics and effects of urban poverty are to be understood and effective action is to be taken. For example, there are few city-level data on child morbidity in low and middle income nations, and even fewer on children's or caregivers' perceptions of their needs and priorities. There are, however, many detailed studies within particular urban neighbourhoods which provide strong evidence of the impacts that urban conditions can have.

Water and Sanitation

Diarrhoeal diseases are still a primary cause of infant and child death for large sections of the world's urban population. Human excreta are the primary source of diarrhoeal disease pathogens. When provision for water and sanitation is poor, diarrhoeal diseases and other diseases linked to contaminated water (such as typhoid) or contaminated food and water (such as cholera and hepatitis A) are among the most serious health problems within urban neighbourhoods – or whole cities.

The impact of diarrhoeal diseases can be considerably underestimated since, when combined with malnutrition (as they often are), they can so weaken the body's defences that diseases such as measles and pneumonia become major causes of child death. Long-term impacts for children are not restricted to health: a city study in Brazil has related early diarrhoeal disease in children to impaired cognitive functioning several years later. An essential factor in ensuring children's health is the availability of safe, sufficient water supplies and provision for sanitation – something frequently absent in poor urban settlements in low and middle income countries.

Too little water is a critical problem, making it impossible to maintain the sanitary conditions essential for preventing endemic disease that contributes so heavily to the death and repeated illness of many children. When water has to be carried or bought by the bottle, many households make do with far less than they need to ensure children's health. In urban Brazil, infants were five times as likely to die in households using public standpipes as in those with water piped to the house. In the absence of adequate supplies of clean water, the maintenance of hygiene during food preparation becomes especially difficult, and this, together with inadequate storage for food, contributes to the likelihood of contamination.

Bottle-fed babies and young children being weaned are at particularly high risk. The impact of inadequate water provision is compounded by the effects of poor sanitation. Only a small proportion of poor urban residents have adequate provision for sanitation, and here too, the problems are not confined to informal settlements. In Azerbaijan, 33 per cent of the urban population still use traditional pit latrines, and another 9. 7 per cent use open pits. Most urban centres in Africa and Asia and many in Latin America have no sewers. Although non-sewered sanitation can work well, the sheer volume and concentration of human waste and waste waters in cities usually make these ineffective.

Where sewers do exist, these are often open, presenting a serious risk to public health. Tens of millions of households in informal settlements only have access to overused and poorly maintained communal or public toilets – one settlement in Kumasi, Ghana, had 320 persons per latrine and long queues were inevitable. Provision for sanitation is so poor in many cities that significant proportions of the population resort to open defecation. The use of public latrines is particularly problematic for young children. Taking a small child any distance to a toilet is impractical, and the darkness, smell and large pit openings in most latrines make their use unpleasant or even frightening for young children.

Evidence from a number of urban settlements indicates that hardly any children under six use these latrines and that in most cases their excrement ends up being thrown into yards, drains or streets, creating a potent source of contamination. Women and adolescent girls may also be reluctant to use public latrines because these facilities afford little or no privacy, and the lack of security increases the risk of these women falling victim to sexual abuse or violence. They face similar problems of privacy and safety when the absence of sanitary facilities forces them to use open land. The absence of drainage and garbage collection contributes further to the likelihood of contamination and disease.

Most informal settlements have no service to collect solid waste. In many African cities, only 10-30 per cent of all urban households' solid wastes are collected, and services are inevitably most deficient for informal settlements. Uncollected garbage, along with excreta, is often dumped in drainage ditches – which can quickly become clogged. When wastewater and storm water cannot be easily drained, flooding spreads waste and excreta widely through the surrounding area. Drainage is an especially serious concern for the many urban communities on steep or swampy land. Children can be at particular risk, since they play wherever there is open land, and may be drawn to wade or play in standing water or to scavenge in piles of garbage. Furthermore, housing built over water-logged sites and linked by poorly constructed wooden walkways in informal settlements is a clear source of danger for small children.

Conditions may improve over time in many illegal or informal settlements through a combination of self-help, mutual cooperation and negotiation with government agencies for some public services. But at best this is a slow and haphazard process. Residents have to negotiate for every kind of infrastructure or service separately. In parts of cities where poorer groups are not living in illegal settlements – for instance in tenement districts – there is generally more provision for infrastructure, but conditions may be as bad as in most informal settlements because maintenance is generally poor and levels of overcrowding extreme.

The impacts of inadequate water, sanitation, drainage and waste removal are not limited to diarrhoeal diseases. Many case studies in low-income settlements have shown the high proportion of children who have debilitating intestinal worm infestations. The prevalence among children of various skin and eye infections such as scabies and trachoma that are associated with a lack of water supplies for washing is also particularly high among those living in poor quality homes and neighbourhoods.

Moreover, malaria, which is often considered a rural disease, is now among the main causes of illness and death among children (and adults) in many urban areas. The occurrence of malaria is often related to poorly drained locations as the *Anopheles* mosquitoes breed on standing water. Similarly, the diseases spread by *Aedes* mosquitoes (including dengue fever, dengue haemorrhagic fever and yellow fever) are related to poor drainage and to inadequate or intermittent water supplies, since these mosquitoes breed in standing water and water containers. Many other disease vectors, including houseflies, fleas, lice and cockroaches, thrive where there is poor drainage and inadequate provision for rubbish collection, sanitation and piped water.

Chemical Pollutants

Although they do not present the same health burden as biological pathogens, toxins and pollutants in water supplies and food, in the air and in unprotected dumps, are a world-wide concern. This is especially the case in urban areas and, disproportionately, in areas inhabited by the poor.

Children are particularly vulnerable to harm from exposure because of their rapid growth and immaturity, both physiologically and metabolically. Lead ingestion is a particular problem for urban children, especially in countries where leaded fuel and paint are still used. In Kaduna, Nigeria, for instance, 92 per cent of children examined had blood lead levels above acceptable limits. In high income nations, exposure occurs predominantly through the ingestion of dust in households containing lead-based paint, a problem particularly in lower income areas with deteriorating housing stock; in the USA, this remains the most common environmental health problem affecting children.

Children are also at risk due to exposure to harmful chemicals, indeed, pesticides are increasingly becoming a source of concern in some inner city areas, where they are used to control roaches, rats and other vermin. The single most significant form of chemical pollutant in terms of children's health in low and middle income countries is indoor air pollution resulting from the use of coal or biomass fuels, poor quality stoves and inadequate ventilation. This is a problem in both rural and urban areas, but one from which children are less likely to have relief outdoors in towns and cities, given the poor quality of the outside air.

All the same, indoor concentrations of pollutants can be many times higher than even the most polluted outdoor air, and infants and young children are often heavily exposed because they remain with their mothers as they cook or undertake other tasks within the home. The effect of these pollutants, combined with malnutrition, may retard growth and increase the incidence of acute respiratory infections. In many cities, the concentration and mix of ambient air pollutants is already high enough to cause illness and premature death for more susceptible individuals.

Worldwide, 1. 5 billion urban dwellers are exposed to ambient air pollution levels that exceed WHO standards – and in many cities, the concentration of pollutants is far above these standards. Some groups are particularly vulnerable: the poorest 'scavenging' families who live and work in city refuse dumps regularly inhale toxic fumes from burning plastic and other dangerous substances. Generally, the prevalence and severity of asthma, along with other respiratory ailments, have increased alarmingly in recent years among urban children.

Reasons are complex and include exposure to urban pollutants, together with allergens and the psychosocial stresses of urban life. Although this phenomenon has been documented chiefly in the high income countries, it is beginning to receive attention in other urban areas. Accidental poisonings are common, especially for one to three year olds, most often from kerosene, household products and medications.

The risk of poisoning is greater in poor quality, overcrowded dwellings where there is no storage space to keep these substances out of reach of children, and where the demands on parents mean that children are not always supervised. Unborn children are also at risk through their mother's expose to chemical pollutants, some of which can cause cancer or birth defects in the foetus or even kill it. Chemicals that are known to harm the foetus by transfer through the placenta include lead, methyl mercury, certain pesticides, PCBs and carbon monoxide. In most low income settlements, however, the developing foetus is more at risk from the mother's nutritional deficiencies or from the impact of parasites and malaria on her health.

Physical Hazards

Millions of urban children around the world are killed every year as a result of preventable injuries that occur within their homes and neighbourhoods, and tens of millions more are seriously injured. Heavy traffic, unprotected stairways and heights, unfinished houses, dangerous house sites, piles of debris and a scarcity of safe play space all expose children to high levels of risk.

The danger of injury increases when tired, overworked caregivers are unable to provide adequate supervision. In countries where infectious and parasitic diseases are well controlled, unintentional injury ranks as the leading cause of death for children, accounting for almost 40 per cent of deaths in the one to 14 age group. In countries where disease and nutritional problems still kill many children, the percentage of injuryrelated deaths is lower but the number of injuries per person is considerably higher, especially in the poorest urban communities.

Most documentation of children's injuries is based on hospital records, but there are good reasons to believe that these provide a very incomplete picture, since most children's injuries are not treated in hospitals, in part because of the expense and the lack of emergency transport. A community-based study in Ibadan, Nigeria, documented 1,236 injuries involving 436 children over three months: these included puncture wounds, lacerations, sprains and dislocations: less than 1 per cent were treated in formal health facilities. In urban and rural areas alike, falls are the single most common cause of injury, especially for younger children. Burns are common for children under four – from hot water or other hot fluids, and from accidents with open fires, stoves or kerosene appliances. High levels of overcrowding increase the likelihood of these events.

A study in a Brazilian squatter settlement focused on 600 children under five, drawing on interviews with mothers. The mothers reported that in the two weeks prior to the interview, 30 per cent of the children had had at least one accident and 12 per cent of these were serious enough to have required care in a clinic or hospital. Falls accounted for 53 per cent of these accidents, followed by cuts (17 per cent) and burns (10 per cent).

Many of the falls were linked to the rough terrain of the settlement. The age of the child was an important determinant of accidents, and peaks in accidents were in the second or fifth years of life. Road accidents are among the most common causes of serious injury in cities in both high and low income countries. But the rapid growth of road traffic in many low income and most middle income nations, along with poorly maintained roads, multiple use of roadways and an absence of sidewalks and safe crossings has contributed to death and injury rates that are much higher than those in Europe or the USA, per road vehicle or passenger-mile.

Access to Entertainments

Urban safety hazards and health risks have a significant effect on the play opportunities available to children. The availability of stimulating, diverse environments that allow them to pretend, experiment and learn are central to optimal development, and have been related to resilience and improved outcomes in high-risk children. Where homes are overcrowded, children may have little choice but to pass much of the day outside, and they can be extraordinarily resourceful in finding opportunities for play within even the most deprived environments – indeed many poor environments are rich in challenge and diversity. But they can also expose children to serious risk, and caregivers often respond by restricting play. As children become more mobile, safety becomes an increasing concern.

In conditions of urban poverty, excreta, broken glass, plastic bags, rotted food and burning materials are common hazards. As children begin to move further from home their range of action and the number of risk factors that they face also increase – traffic in particular, but also stray dogs, standing water, open drains and debrisfilled lots. Older children are more capable of identifying hazards, but the drive to play and explore and an enjoyment of risk-taking can override the need for caution. As a result, injury rates remain fairly constant throughout childhood, while the kinds of injuries tend to change with age. Girls are generally at lower risk – a function of the greater restrictions imposed upon them.

Opportunities for play are also restricted in high-income nations countries, where spaces for recreation in urban areas are often limited or, increasingly, involve a financial cost, while motor vehicles make streets hazardous for play and open areas are used for parking. Moreover, parents' working patterns, the distance between home and school and the growing use of the car mean that, outside school hours, many children are isolated in their homes and separated from their peers. This isolation may be heightened by parents' concern for the safety of their children in urban areas.

Housing

Many children's rights are rooted in the fundamental human right to decent, secure, affordable housing. Survival, health and optimal development are related to the quality of housing and its surroundings; access to livelihoods, schooling and other services are determined by its location; emotional security, family stability and even the quality of community relations are tied to security of tenure.

But the urban poor struggle with housing – getting it, keeping it and coping with its inadequacies. In most cities in low and middle income nations, between 25 and 50 per cent of the population live in illegally built settlements. The quality of housing in these settlements is generally poor and often wretched, made of wood and plastic scavenged from dumps. This is a result not only of low incomes, but also of the reluctance of households to invest because of the uncertainty that they will be permitted to stay.

The location of informal settlements has a logic – they are concentrated in dangerous areas because the more dangerous the site, the greater the chance the residents can avoid eviction. The illegal settlements in a city often coincide with the areas most at risk from flooding or tidal inundation or landslides. Similarly, the most poorly constructed housing is also the most prone to severe earthquake damage, as testified by recent devastating quakes in the Colombian town of Armenia, the Turkish towns of Adapazari, Golcuk, Istanbul and Izmit, and Ahmedabad and Bhuj in the Indian state of Gujurat.

In many cities, poor groups also live in large concentrations in dilapidated, over-crowded inner city tenements and boarding houses: in these cases there is a trade-off between the far higher costs that households incur, for example with regard to rent and overcrowding, and the advantages provided by the location in terms of access to services and jobs. Furthermore, such problems are by no means restricted to low-income countries. Most poor people in urban areas in the USA, for instance, face serious housing problems, including rents that can exceed 50 per cent of their incomes.

An unknown number – but certainly tens of millions – of the world's urban children and adults are actually homeless and sleep in public places (pavements, stations, parks, graveyards) or construction sites and work places. In central Mumbai (formerly Bombay), India, more than a hundred thousand people live on pavements, half of them children, because incomes are insufficient to allow them to live even in cheap peripheral areas. Homelessness is predominantly an urban phenomenon, in part because of the commercialisation of land and housing markets in the world's cities.

Even in high income countries, research confirms that homelessness among families with children is increasing despite the recent years of affluence. The experience results in anxiety and depression for both children and parents, and can lead to the break up of families, as children are placed in foster care. In New York City, 60 per cent of residents in shelters for adults had children who could not be with them.

Even when poor urban families are securely housed, their housing is seldom adequate to support their children's survival, development and the highest attainable standard of health. Numerous hazards are posed by flimsy shelters on disaster-prone land.

Accidental fires are common in areas with highly inflammable building materials, and are rendered still more serious by the lack or inadequacy of emergency services. In other cases, fires can be deliberately set to drive households off the land they have occupied. In high-income countries, fires are also related to poor housing conditions, but more often to faulty wiring, defective heating equipment and the absence of smoke alarms.

There are also numerous health risks associated with poor quality housing construction and materials. Lack of screens exposes children to flies and mosquitoes, and porous walls and roofing harbour rodents and insect pests. Hard to clean floors increase contact with pathogens – the agents that cause disease – especially for babies and young children. Poor living environments, including noise and crowding, have long been recognised to generate stress, to undermine coping strategies, interfere with social relationships and contribute to physical and mental illness. In high-income nations, overcrowding is measured by rooms per person; in low-income nations by persons per room.

Three or more persons per room is common among poor urban populations, amounting to one or two square metres of space per person. There are particular effects for children. In several countries, including India and the USA, noise and overcrowding have been related to poor cognitive development, behavioural problems, lower motivation, delayed psychomotor development, and difficulties with parents, including child abuse.

Many of these outcomes have been related more generally to poor housing quality. Poor quality, overcrowded housing also favours the transmission of acute respiratory infections, which are the single largest cause of infant and child death in most low and middle income nations. Although these infections are by no means an urban phenomenon, they tend to be more prevalent in urban areas, as the frequency of contact, the density of the population and the concentration and proximity of both infectious and susceptible people promote disease transmission. And, with limited health and financial resources, a child who contracts bronchitis or pneumonia in low and middle income nations is 50 times more likely to die than a child in Europe or North America. Overcrowding is also a risk factor for the transmission of many other diseases that affect children, including diarrhoea and tuberculosis.

Evictions

Millions of urban dwellers around the world live in fear of eviction. In the case of illegal settlements, even those on undesirable land are at risk. A household survey in six wards of Dar-es-Salaam, Tanzania, in 1998 found that between 10 and 20 per cent of households had been evicted in the previous year. A review of 40 eviction cases from around the world between 1980 and 1993 found that eight involved more than 100,000 persons; the largest involved 720,000 people evicted in Seoul, South Korea in preparation for the Olympic Games. This was not a one time event; between 1960 and 1990, 5 million people were evicted from their homes in Seoul, many of them several times, often from sites provided after previous evictions. Of course, housing security is not just an economic and political issue.

The impact of eviction upon children can be particularly devastating. Evictions usually lead to homelessness and almost always to major economic upheaval. Possessions may be destroyed, family stability jeopardised, livelihoods and schooling threatened and social networks undermined. Children involved describe the violence, panic and confusion of the evictions and the experience of sleeping rough afterwards and being separated from friends. They also face the difficulties in re-establishing a stable life and frequent breakdowns in family relations as a consequence of the stress and economic difficulties.

Evictions or displacement also arise from armed conflict, political violence, natural disasters and other emergencies that affect millions of adults and children each year, and often result in children being separated from their family. This can mean streams of refugees or displaced rural dwellers flooding into cities where housing is already at a premium. These displaced people are often resented by other urban dwellers. This is especially so if they are undocumented immigrants who often live in constant fear of discovery and forced repatriation. Children from 'illegal' or 'unwelcome' communities are highly vulnerable to prejudice, harassment, attack and incarceration, especially when they are forced to work for survival.

Social Dimensions Urban Life

In deprived urban areas where local governance is ineffective, resources are scarce and poorly distributed, communities empowerment is undeveloped, participatory channels are inexistent and support structures are weak, the impact of poverty on the child, the family and the fabric of society can be devastating. These outcomes are further compounded by difficulties associated with the physical environment in poor urban areas.

Inevitably, challenging living conditions undermine the capacity to provide optimal care for children. Overburdened caregivers are far more likely to have to leave children unsupervised or to cut corners in the many procedures that are necessary for healthy living – managing water supplies, keeping children clean, preparing and storing food hygienically and dealing with waste and excreta in the absence of adequate services. For example, reduced cooking times are thought to be connected with the retention of toxicity in boiled cassava meal, a staple food in many parts of Africa, especially when combined with a protein-deficient diet. Even high levels of parental knowledge about health, hygiene and safety cannot guarantee that children will be well provided for in very poor conditions. Heavy demands on caregivers in combination with long distances to work and the absence of viable alternatives can mean that there is no good source of care for many young children for long hours every day. Often the burden of care in households falls upon girls, who are left to look after their siblings while parents work.

The psychological stresses imposed by living in poor urban conditions also take their toll. Caregivers in crowded and chaotic conditions have been found to be less responsive to their children, and more restrictive, controlling and punitive. Under the many pressures of poverty this can escalate to abuse and neglect. When resources are scarce and mothers or child carers are faced with a heavy domestic workload or are forced to work long hours outside the home, one result can be malnutrition. This condition contributes to more than half of all child deaths, to chronic illness and to a slowing of development on all fronts. It also undermines children's immune defences and increases their vulnerability to disease.

Young children during breastfeeding or weaning are particularly vulnerable, but there is also a risk for older children who are often given cheap food or sweets sold by street vendors or local shops. Urban price differentials may also mean that poor families have difficulty finding or affording fresh products, another contributory factor to poor diets. The problem can be compounded by unsanitary environments: sanitation- related diseases cause decreased food intake, impaired nutrient absorption and direct nutrient losses through vomiting and diarrhoea, while parasitic infestations can absorb a significant percentage of a child's nutrient intake, as well as interfering with digestion and absorption. Data from

84 countries indicate that the best predictor of nutritional status, next to financial access to food, is the level of access to water. Recent figures demonstrate that, even without disaggregating for income, urban children in low and middle income nations are between one and two standard deviations below the international median in terms of height for age.

The difficulty of providing adequate care for children in poor households can be exacerbated in urban areas by the breakdown of family units and the frequent lack of social support. Many observers have pointed to the relatively high numbers of urban households headed by single mothers around the world as a factor explaining poor outcomes for children. There is no question that female-headed households are disproportionately poor, or that it takes more effort on the part of a single adult to provide high quality care for children. However, there is also evidence that women are more likely to invest their limited resources in children's well-being and long-term success, and that many children do better in female-headed households.

Urban Neighbourhoods

Many poor urban children live in rundown inner cities, peripheral squatter communities or barren suburbs where their social, cultural and recreational needs receive little attention. In four Johannesburg neighbourhoods, children described settings almost completely lacking in appealing possibilities. There were no recreational facilities, nor any safe places to play or see friends. Parks and empty lots were taken over by drunk, abusive adults and filled with refuse.

Swimming pools were too far away and too expensive to use. Mobility was limited by heavy traffic, crumbling sidewalks and broken traffic lights. The bus service was patchy and unaffordable, and streets were so poorly lit that children were afraid to go out at night. Aside from the lack of opportunity, children find the stigma of living in such rundown and marginal communities to be a serious issue. Far from taking their physical environments for granted, children are extremely sensitive to their surroundings, finding them a source of satisfaction but also a cause for humiliation and distress. Neighbourhood quality, accessibility and opportunity for children and adolescents are determined to some degree by the level of formal municipal provision.

But local community institutions like churches, cultural centres and recreational clubs also play a significant role, and they depend on the level of social organisation and commitment within a community. Many African-American churches in major cities of the US have taken initiatives to mobilise community members to plan and manage their own neighbourhoods, but research in the USA has also indicated that this kind of neighbourhood resource base tends to be weaker where there are high concentrations of poverty, joblessness and residential mobility. These same factors have also been related to higher levels of violence and insecurity. In cities around the world community violence has become an increasingly commonplace part of children's experience.

Exposure to violence has repeatedly been linked to higher rates of depression, anxiety, distress, aggression and behavioural disturbances for children and adolescents. There seems to be little doubt, moreover, that poverty and the inadequate living conditions, insecurity and marginalisation experienced by many poor communities can feed frustration and aggresssion. In one high poverty neighbourhood in Chicago, 47 per cent of girls and 55 per cent of boys between 7 and 13 had reportedly seen someone being shot or stabbed, and over

20 per cent lived with someone who had been shot. In Washington DC, 75 per cent of a sample of African American elementary school children had witnessed violence in their communities, ranging from physical assaults and gang violence to rape and homicide. Almost half their parents were unaware that they had been exposed to any violence.

Children and adolescents may not only be victims of violence, but also contribute to it. Bullying by peers is a problem for many children, and vandalism, drug use and gang-related crime by young people are the cause of fear and concern in communities around the world. These activities may, in turn, bring children into contact with law enforcement officials. In certain cases where the juvenile justice system is weak or non-existent, children become subject to arbitrary treatment by the police or to other rights abuses. In part at least, phenomena such as vandalism can be related to boredom and the lack of opportunity and hope. In many communities the provision of recreational facilities, job training and options for constructive involvement have resulted in dramatic reductions in crime and gang violence.

Schooling and Work

Schooling, like most other basic services, tends to be more readily available to urban children than their rural counterparts. But school remains either inaccessible or unaffordable for many poor urban children. Moreover, the general quality of schools in poor urban areas can be extremely low, and this constitutes yet another disincentive for parents and children. Especially in illegal settlements, governments may overlook their obligation to provide education or, indeed, any other service. When the large Basic Education for Hard to Reach Urban Children project was developed for children in hazardous labour in Bangladesh, it was quickly discovered that more than half the children attending these small learning centres in slum areas were not 'working children', indicating that there was a more general problem with access to schooling. But even when government schools are within walking distance, many urban children do not attend. Of those that do enrol, many drop out in the first few years. Door-to-door surveys in poor neighbourhoods in Hyderabad and Secunderabad indicate that the quality of schools and of teaching is a major factor.

Overcrowded and rundown classrooms, disinterested teachers, physical punishment, social discrimination and humiliation are some of the reasons cited by parents and children for their lack of motivation over time. In the case of particularly vulnerable groups, such as children with disabilities, the social and physical barriers to attending school in poor urban areas can be insurmountable without special support and provisions.

Many children are denied their right to education in order to undertake household or domestic chores, or to care for younger siblings. This is as true for rural areas as it is for urban ones, but the lack of public utilities and services in many poor urban communities contributes to inappropriate burdens for millions of children, especially girls.

Other children may be withdrawn from school to contribute to household income. A survey in a Kolkata (Calcutta) 'slum' revealed that 84 per cent of school age children were not attending school, and that of these, 49 per cent were working outside the home – as rag pickers, domestic helpers, leather workers or battery breakers. Child labour not only impacts upon educational opportunities, it can also take dangerous and degrading forms. There is probably no city in the world where there are not some children exposed to hazardous work, but the proportion of children in this position is particularly high in many low and middle income nations where, for instance, they make a living picking through waste or working with dangerous machinery, heat, toxic chemicals and dust.

Domestic labour in the homes of others is especially prevalent in urban areas, often involving children sent from rural areas, and entailing long hours, little or no pay, little relief from isolation and, frequently, abusive treatment and sexual violence. An especially serious violation of children's rights is child prostitution, a phenomenon that is particularly associated with major cities with high levels of poverty.

A recent estimate from UNICEF in India indicates that there are more than 100,000 child prostitutes in that country's five major cities. In Mexico, a study of the cities of Acapulco, Cancún, Cuidad Juarez, Guadalajara, Tapachula and Tijuana estimated that a total of 4,600 children are sexually exploited in these cities, while some 16,000 are believed to be exploited at the national level. This, in turn, exposes these children to violence, exploitation and sexually transmitted diseases, including HIV/AIDS. The fact that in Thailand close to $300 million is estimated to be transferred annually from urban to rural areas by women working in the sex trade in urban areas helps to illustrate the direct link between poverty and prostitution in a rural-urban context.

Status of Street Children

The phenomenon of children living on the street is a peculiarly urban one, although many of the children involved may originate from rural areas. The demands of work for some urban children push them onto city streets for many hours a day, and in some of these cases links with home can become tenuous. In other cases, work may be secondary, and children may have left home because of abuse, a desire for excitement or relief from oppressive home conditions.

At night, these children become particularly vulnerable to all forms of abuse. During winter, cold can be a deadly enemy: in Moscow, where there are estimated to be 50,000 homeless children, many sleep on air vents for the metro system to escape the freezing temperatures, or even risk disease in the city's sewers in order to find relative warmth. A large proportion of children on the street engage in hazardous work – dodging traffic as they sell goods to passing motorists for instance.

Many are involved in legitimate work; others choose or are pushed into illegal activity, engaging in petty crime and theft, working in the commercial sex or drug trade or becoming drawn into organised begging or rag-picking rackets. Whether or not they are breaking the law, these children are among the most stigmatised urban dwellers, constantly facing abuse from other citizens and harassment by the police. Often children are arrested for crimes or simply for vagrancy, and can be trapped for long months in the slow moving bureaucracy of the justice system, detained in conditions that violate their basic rights.

Welfare Activities for Urban Children

Addressing the problems outlined in earlier is a significant challenge, yet there are hundreds of precedents, many supported by UNICEF, that demonstrate how much can be achieved, even with limited resources, to promote local governance in favour of children's rights and to translate the commitments arising from the ratification of the CRC at the municipal level. And there are compelling reasons why putting children first is in the interest of the entire urban population. First and foremost, children's healthy development and their active participation in society are crucial to the future of every city and urban settlement, indeed the state of children living in urban areas is an effective barometer of social progress. Second, children are particularly sensitive to the conditions in which they live and are especially vulnerable to the effects of poverty, poor housing, environmental pollution and exposure to violence, abuse and neglect.

Third, failing children brings huge costs to societies – urban and rural alike. When children's growth and development are compromised, so too is their potential to evolve in their capacities and talents, to assume responsibilities and promote economic and social progress in the world's urban settlements. Given both their potential and their vulnerability, government action (or lack of action) can have a significant impact upon children.

At the local level, urban administrations and municipalities have an instrumental role to play in protecting children, ensuring their healthy development and providing constructive outlets for their energy and creativity. Given this, it is important that innovative strategies and mechanisms are developed and implemented to ensure a new political culture in which efforts made by communities and civil society are articulated through local government activities. Where mechanisms for information exchange exist, these innovations can easily be shared with and, when relevant, replicated by other cities and communities.

But if local government initiatives are to be effective, action and support at the national level are crucial. National action to promote local governance for children's rights includes the ratification and implementation of the most relevant human rights conventions, especially the CRC; the development of a constitutional framework protective of human rights; the establishment of participatory democratic institutions that promote social inclusion for low income groups; the promotion of a process of decentralisation of responsibilites; the provision of adequate resources to enable effective action on the part of local government, and the presence of a strong and independent judiciary to ensure effective law enforcement. Together, these elements provide the political, economic and legal underpinnings for effective local actions and help constitute a framework for the good governance that is crucial to the realisation of children's rights.

Many significant steps towards establishing or furthering good urban governance have been taken in urban settlements around the world. This Digest looks in particular at initiatives to:

— Promote the role of children in urban governance

— Improve physical and social conditions for children and their families.

— Of course, these two sets of initiatives are not independent: facilitating and supporting children's participation is one of the best ways of focusing upon key physical and social interventions to improve urban living conditions.

The Convention on the Rights of the Child offers urban authorities a framework within which to make real progress towards realising children's rights. On a practical level, and within an urban context, a commitment to the CRC can be translated through, among other things:

— the development of city-wide children's rights strategies, providing the framework for policy action, promoting the coordination of activities among relevant actors and identifying concrete goals and targets to promote and monitor progress and encourage the broad engagement of civil society;

- the establishment of local government structures that mainstream children's interests in local plans and policies;
- the incorporation of children's concerns, and particularly those of children belonging to the most vulnerable groups, in local budgets;
- the development of periodic 'state of the city's children' reports to review progress and advance the cause of children.

Promoting children's rights in an urban context challenges local governments to be flexible and to adapt their organisational structure to meet local needs, and there are already many examples of cities in which this challenge is being met. In Croatia, for example, the Towns and Districts Friends of Children initiative launched in 1999 sees local authorities and civil society, children's institutions, parents and children working together to make their towns and districts more child friendly and to monitor achievements through a sophisticated set of indicators based on children's rights. In Bolivia, 109 municipalities have adopted a common strategy that involves families directly and that aims at reducing child and maternal mortality, advocating for children's rights and increasing community participation. In Ukraine, mayors from 35 cities, along with representatives of youth organisations and mass media met in 2000 in order to develop local plans of action and observe best practices in favour of children.

Child Participation in Governance

One of the key characteristics of good local governance for children is founded on the rights of children to express their views freely, and to seek, receive and impart information (articles 12 and 13 of the CRC). Participation is a process in which children and youth engage with other people around issues that concern their individual and collective life conditions. In this process, the child experiences him or herself as playing a useful role in the community. Participants interact in ways that respect each other's dignity, with the intention of achieving a shared goal. Formal processes of participation deliberately create structures for children's engagement in constructing meaning and sharing decision making.

One of the longest-running examples of children's participation is the Growing Up in Cities project pioneered in the 1970s, which aims to understand the reasons why young people find their city a good place in which to grow up, or a place where they feel alienated and disconnected. With support from UNESCO's MOST Programme, the project has recently completed an indepth study of children's participation in eight cities around the world.

Many other projects now recognise the value of involving children. For example, concern over the living conditions in Harare's informal settlements promted Save the Children (UK) and a local partner organisation (Inter Country People's Aid) to carry out a situation analysis in two of these settlements in 1998. While the results were useful, the researchers involved realised that the findings had failed to reflect the reality for children, and local children themselves complained that their voices had been marginalised and that adults who had spoken on their behalf were often poorly informed about their real situation, perceptions and wishes.

Save the Children responded by devising a more extensive and participatory project, where the researchers were children themselves from informal settlements. The results of this research have subsequently been used to help create a network of organisations working in informal settlements, to develop programmes of assistance based on the problems identified by the children and to raise the profile of the communities involved among various levels of government and the general public. Moreover, the experience brought to the children involved an increased sense of confidence and self-esteem. Recognising the right of children to participate and express their views in all matters affecting them, many city governments have now begun to involve children and youth in discussions of their priorities. Brazil provides an interesting example in this regard: in the city of Barra Mansa child counsellors elected by their peers not only monitor the policies and resource allocations of the city government, but also determine priorities for spending part of the city's investment funds.

In Ecuador, several city authorities have involved children in defining criteria for assessing the city. In 15 communities in the capital, Quito, children's brigades, supported by trained youth leaders, identified what they regarded as the most pressing problems and promoted action to address these.

In Albania, UNICEF is supporting a Youth Parliament Project that aims to promote youth participation in public debates. Representative assemblies for children between 14 and 18 years were established in six of the country's prefectures. Two hundred democratically elected young parliamentarians prepare youth action agendas, learn about civic affairs through partnership with municipal and national officials, present plans of action to municipal government and conduct peer-to-peer education programmes. The programme is currently being extended to reach all 12 of Albania's prefectures. In Ukraine there is a Children's Parliamentarian Movement in 15 cities.

Child Friendly Cities Movement

The potential for action by urban governments on children's rights and for children to participate in and contribute to the decisions that effect their life has led to the development of the Child Friendly Cities movement. While there is no single definition of a Child Friendly City, the unifying principle is that a city is considered friendly when it is able to assure the rights of its children. A Child Friendly City legislates and enforces ordinances consistent with the Convention on the Rights of the Child, and gives priority to children, especially in the provision of basic services and the allocation of resources.

The goal of the initiative is to reach all urban children, not least those who are poor and excluded, and to promote new ways of doing this, including the participation of children. To achieve this, the Child Friendly City initiative encourages national governments and supports urban authorities to provide the necessary legal policy and institutional framework. The Child-Friendly concept has taken root in urban areas around the world.

In Malaysia, for example, a Charter on Making Urban Areas Child-Friendly was developed after a national conference on children's rights: its 'ten strategic actions' are aimed specifically at urban local authorities. This has been complemented by a child friendly survey instrument that involves the participation of children in assessing their own urban environments and the compilation of a book on action-oriented activities.

In the Dominican Republic, an initiative was started in 2000 to develop Child Friendly Municipalities, with the aim of strengthening the planning and administrative capacity of these political units. The initiative started with seven pilot municipalities, but after only 18 months,

35 of the country's 118 municipal councils were taking part. Achievements have included the establishment of three training centres for facilitators who will in turn lead training activities for child friendly local governance at the municipal level. Training packages have also been developed for candidates for municipal public office, and training manuals and a regular journal are produced to reinforce training content. These efforts have been supported by the national authority which is committed to decentralising responsibilities and budgets and to taking on new tasks within a child rights perspective. In Italy, guidance and support for the numerous Child Friendly City initiatives is provided by the Ministry for the Environment.

Under the title of 'Sustainable Cities for Children', this programme encourages local governments to adopt a special code, including the collection of indicators that monitor the city's quality of life from children's perspectives. Innovations implemented by different local authorities are shared in yearly fora, with prizes presented to the cities judged to have performed best. Initiatives have included community and child participation in urban planning, an emphasis on quality and accessibility to public spaces for play and socialisation, child-centred urban planning and management methods and making services child-friendly.

In South Africa, the city of Johannesburg is the first major urban centre to make a commitment to implementing the Convention on the Rights of the Child at the local level. The Johannesburg initiative will be used as a pilot project for this process, which will unfold throughout the country between 2002 and 2006.

In addition to structures that promote children's participation, effective action for and with children relies on the availability of current and accurate data.

Governments and agencies, whether at the local, national or international level, cannot address the needs of deprived or excluded children if they lack information on who these children are, where they live and in what conditions. Interesting inititiatives in this area include the establishment of a local information system for monitoring children's rights in Ecuador.

This system produces information on demography, employment, family income, migration, health, nutrition, breastfeeding, education, child development and water and sanitation. The data are gathered through the active participation of the National Census and Statistics Institute with support from local communities. Dhaka City Corporation uses a geographic information system to map urban basic service delivery, and in Moscow, the City Government has given its support to the establishment of a city database on street children, who had previously been invisible in urban statistics. Other new and relevant approaches for understanding urban conditions include city-wide mapping of housing conditions and health outcomes, and accurate, detailed 'slum' and 'shack' censuses undertaken by organisations of the urban poor. There are also many examples of neighbourhood or district maps developed by and with children that have provided local governments and other local agencies with the means to address children's needs and promote respect for their rights.

4

Social Work in Slums

The extension of slums in developing countries is a product of 20th- and 21st century urban growth and represents the very essence of the Third World city. Attempts have been made to eliminate slums but they have almost universally failed because they do not question the urban model that generates the slum in the first place. In our own analysis of these causes, we suggest a three-track approach that requires taking into account citizens' demands and needs; evaluating the available resources; and, finally, implementing urban governance in a way that fosters collective interests. To advance in this path it is necessary to promote a participatory approach in both social and political terms, adapted to the specific spatial and social context of each city.

The slum is characterised by the precarious nature of its habitat. But it is much more than that: it can genuinely be seen as a 'hothouse' of cultural creativity, economic invention and social innovation. Classic urban planning principles are based on comprehensive planning regarding land allocation, infrastructural organisation, and decisions on technical services and networks. In the slums, however, this technocratic approach is undermined by the social practices of individuals, families and social groups, particularly the poorer ones.

These actors resort to their own emergency solutions to urban integration problems, and they do so at the micro-level at which these problems are posed – generally the plot of land, the house, then the district. In most cases the result is an individual or family construction on a plot of land which is occupied either illegally or by informal agreement, without being connected to the customary utilities. Although poor citizens recognise the importance of infrastructures and urban services for their wellbeing, they do not consider them a minimum requirement to move in. The immediate consequences of this situation are:

— for the users: buildings are of inadequate quality, town districts have poor infrastructure, equipment and collective services, and suffer various forms of environmental degradation;
— for urban planners, it becomes impossible to apply classical models of spatial organisation. It also becomes necessary to improvise remedial solutions based on existing social and territorial conditions.

This discrepancy may lead to two opposing tendencies: the denial of the 'social fact' by urban planners and the corresponding implementation of a repressive policy aiming to destroy whatever infrastructure or housing has been created outside official regulations and standards, and; the establishment of alternative policies aiming to reorganise and rehabilitate slum areas on the basis of what the resident communities have undertaken themselves.

The question of land ownership is one of the fundamental issues regarding slums in developing countries. In many poor areas of the city most people do not own the land on which they have built their house. In certain cases customary forms of land occupancy still exist, and the plot is allotted to a family by the local community. On rare occasions, this solution is legally recognised by the state. Generally though, land occupancy is wilfully ignored in favour of existing administrative, financial and regulatory procedures, often based on Western legislation imposed during the colonial era.

It has been estimated that between 25 and 70 per cent of urban dwellers in the developing countries live in irregular settlements. Secure land tenure is thus one of the major problems facing local and national authorities in these countries. For the United Nations, secure land tenure is a key element for the integration of the urban poor, as is their recognition by the public authorities. It can also encourage families to invest into upgrading their plots and diversify their use. This gives them protection against possible evictions and provides them with an asset that may serve as a guarantee in certain markets (e.g. for the purpose of acquiring bank loans).

Nevertheless, the solutions are not cut and dried: legal versus illegal, formality versus informality. They will depend on the political will of the authorities, the lobbying and negotiating capacities of the affected populations and on the innovative measures implemented to regulate land ownership. This perhaps lies at the crux of the problem: the vast majority of the urban poor suffer precarious forms of territorial integration, leaving much scope for conflicts between urban investors and the social needs of local inhabitants.

Land ownership is not of course the only issue that bedevils the poor residents of the cities in the South: access to collective services and infrastructures is an indispensable part of all urban integration policies. The poor are poor because they also have difficulty accessing urban services; moreover, when they finally obtain this right its cost is proportionally higher than for other urban groups. Following the recent evaluation of the United

Nations on the Millennium Development Goals, access to clean drinking water and to wastewater treatment facilities has improved during the past 10 years. But although the situation in urban areas is better than in rural regions, the problems are by and large similar: collective facilities and major infrastructures (roads and water) are inadequate, the socio-spatial distribution of services is selective, public-private partnerships are applied in an incoherent manner, administrative and financial management is inefficient, and maintenance is poor.

In the past, public policies have aimed at eradicating slums, without taking into account the potential of their inhabitants to resolve the very problems that slums reputedly generate. Especially in the contemporary era of globalisation, it is important to stress the resources that slums can offer the 'chaotic' city. This requires a reassessment of views on urbanisation. Sustainable urban development will only be possible if we concentrate on solving the problems of the majority of urban populations in ways that make use of their own creativity and involve them in decision-making.

According to a whole range of material, natural and socio-economic indicators on developing countries, spatial and demographic urban growth is characterised by the deterioration of physical, economic and social living conditions for a large and increasing part of the urban population. It is argued that there is a need to reconsider certain established approaches. On the one hand, there is an exclusively sectoral, technological and local approach which posits a 'radiant future' for every poor city neighbourhood in the Third World, a future consisting mainly of better provision of water and sanitary services. On the other hand, a more realistic approach that accepts that, although the policies and plans of governments and international organisations may reflect a true commitment to solving the problems of the poor in urban areas, they are often ill-advised or wrongly conceived.

Against this backdrop, local, national and international policies have steadily evolved from repressive approaches aiming to eradicate slums and control the 'undesirable dwellers' to an assimilating view of the urban populations. From this stance, in its role as facilitator the state offers services and acts as a coordinator of policies and actions in the urban sphere. At best this strategy has resulted in improved legislation, collective infrastructure and services. At worst, however, it has tended to exacerbate corruption, and has forced the poor to become micro-entrepreneurs and become responsible for their own livelihoods. However desirable some aspects of this transition may be, it means that the majority of the urban poor are still living in highly vulnerable circumstances.

In a context of globalisation and of economic and political liberalisation, the result of such policies has been the impoverishment of poorer sections of the population, the explosive growth of the number and size of cities, and ever more complex and costly problems that need to be addressed. The innovative solutions proposed are too often unsustainable, and there is an apparent incapacity to go beyond orthodox planning and management approaches. This is in spite of the widespread acknowledgement that resolving the 'urban problem' in the developing countries is crucial.

Slum and Urban Growth

The slum question is not marginal to urban development – it is at its very heart. Urban growth takes place primarily in developing countries in which populations move from rural to urban regions at a very fast pace.

According to UN-Habitat, 'some 923,986,000 people, or 32% of the world's total urban population, live in slums; some 43% of the urban population of all developing regions combined live in slums; some 78% of the urban population in the least developed countries live in slums; some 6% of the urban population in developed regions live in slum-like conditions'. The total number of slum dwellers in the world increased by about 36 per cent during the 1990s, and in the next 30 years the global number of slum dwellers will increase to about two billion if no concerted action to address the challenge of slums is taken.

In both territorial and demographic terms, the world is becoming more and more urban. This process now affects above all the developing countries in Asia and Africa, and Latin America to a somewhat lesser degree (where the level of urbanisation is already exceedingly high). The rate of urban growth in many countries in the South continues to be high, and invariably leads to a serious degradation of living conditions for the majority of city dwellers. The figures quoted in the UN study speak for themselves: depending on the level of poverty in each country, between two and four city dwellers out of five live in slums, with significant consequences for their own lives and the lives of coming generations: precarious conditions for them, uncertainty for their offspring.

The scale of the urban-rule shift is more perceivable if looked at in historical perspective. In 1800 a mere three per cent of the world's population lived in an urban environment, a proportion that rose to 14 per cent in 1900 and to 30 per cent in 1950. In the year 2000, 47 per cent, that is, almost half of the 6,055 million inhabitants of the world were city dwellers – 76 per cent in the developed countries and 40 per cent in the less developed ones. Globally, this proportion is likely to reach 60 per cent by

2030, due primarily to urbanisation in the developing world. This trend goes hand in hand with an explosion of metropolitan centres of over one million inhabitants. Worldwide, there were 12 such cities in 1900, 83 in 1950, and 411 in 2000. Nevertheless, in 2003 the United Nations Population Division confirmed that a majority of the current three billion city dwellers – who will become five billion by 2030 – still live in small or medium-sized urban agglomerations. In the developing countries, 16 per cent of the population live in a megalopolis of over five million inhabitants, 24 per cent in a metropolis of one to five million, 9.4 per cent in an agglomeration of 500,000 to one million inhabitants, and 50.5 per cent in cities of less than 500,000 inhabitants.

Confronted with this demographic and territorial revolution, urban decision makers are often placed in a very difficult, if not impossible, situation. Sometimes this is due to a lack of political will, but more often it is the result of a lack of financial resources.

Living Conditions of Urban Poor

The precarious conditions in the developing countries should not blind us to the fact that poverty, environmental deterioration and social segregation are by no means only to be found in the poorest countries on our planet. Such a view would overlook major aspects of urban history, and socio-spatial disparities that even today cause Western cities to tolerate poverty zones. Using household waste as an example, Lieberherr reminded us that between the 12th and the 19th centuries unsanitary conditions prevailed in the French capital without causing a particular outcry among the citizens. Similarly, in his novel Water Music North-American writer T.C. Boyle describes London's poor districts in 1795, at the time that Scots explorer Mungo Park discovered the African kingdom of Se′gou. At the end of the 18th century the British capital was very much like the most depressed areas of contemporary cities in the Third World.

Urban poverty in the industrialised countries is not only a historical fact –undeniably, it is still with us. An article in the Monde Diplomatique informed readers that the Portuguese government had just launched a special relocation program, earmarked at over one billion euro, in which 150,000 persons living in 'barracas' between Lisbon and Porto were to move to more adequate housing.

Although as stated by Ruffin, most slum-dwellers live in the urban agglomerations of developing countries, it is estimated that six per cent of urban dwellers in the rich countries live under extremely precarious conditions, while public expenditure for subsidised housing and urban rehabilitation is spiralling downward. Further shortages and even more precarious living conditions may be feared as a result.

This makes it clear that regardless of the city or region of the world, poverty and precarious habitat are intimately connected. The French Institute of Statistics and Economics has confirmed this in France via its definitions and urban poverty indicators: a concentration of low-income households, over-population, a lack of basic material comforts, territorial localisation, poor transport networks and access to urban services. Studies conducted in Canada during the 1990s also confirm the link between poverty and urban phenomena.

Poverty increased significantly between 1990 and 1995, going from 4.2 to 5.5 million people, primarily in urban areas. Most poor citizens live in the city centres, where the main economic activities are concentrated. This is due to the types of housing they have access to, and to the facilities provided by the proximity of public services. Ruffin estimates that in France approximately one million households are inadequately housed, or have no housing at all. Although the official discourse revolves around the fight against poverty and social disparities, funding for subsidised houses is being cut. The practices of social segregation and spatial fragmentation best explain these developments, and they are universally applicable. The truth is that the trend towards discriminatory and inequitable urbanisation is found everywhere, in both rich countries and poor ones.

Strategic Planning for Slums

The 'urban question' is thus clearly multi-faceted and multi-dimensional. The various research projects and urban development activities that have been implemented by the Swiss Federal Institute of Technology, Lausanne (EPFL) for nearly 20 years in Latin America, Africa and Asia have made us receptive to the plural and association-based approach to urban planning at different levels: intraurban, urban-rural, regional-national-world. We also feel it is fundamental to acknowledge fully the contributions of specific players and take into account the opinions of a plethora of professional groups.

A scientific cooperation project between Vietnamese and Swiss social scientists, engineers and architects that lasted almost eight years deepened our understanding of the interactions between precarious habitats, poverty, social exclusion and spatial planning. The Vietnam project established a link between the natural and the man-made environment, highlighting two dimensions which provide a better understanding of urban slums. This type of research activity aiming at providing innovative policies and urban programmes corresponding to the needs of a majority of citizens was the focus of a project funded by the Swiss Agency for Development and Cooperation (SDC). In cooperation with the Bolivian Ministry for Urban Affairs, a team headed by the Swiss Federal Institute of Technology in Lausanne attempted to put into practice a presidential decision to supply subsidised housing for the poorest citizens. Two facts symptomatic of the difficulties which confronted urban dwellers in Bolivia at the time: the informal urban sector caused by macro-economic changes grew from 43 per cent in 1976 to 55 per cent in 1987; and, in 1992, a CEPAL study estimated that there was a shortage of some 270,000 housing units. Instead of asking the population to adapt to existing regulations and institutions, the research project took the opposite stance and asked the questions: 'Who are these urban poor in need of housing?', 'What conditions do they live in?', and 'What are their aspirations and what are they willing to do to improve their situation?'.

A group of experts, including representatives from academia, finance, the government and civil society attempted to answer these questions in two steps: first by looking directly at people's socio-economic and housing conditions; then, by examining the reasons for the malfunctioning of an existing public housing credit system that marginalises those without a fixed salary, particularly low-income families. The conclusion reached was that a change of perspective was required: it was necessary to find financial backers prepared to grant credit on a different basis, adapting them to the reimbursement capacity of the parties in question and to the speed with which they could execute construction. This kind of participatory logic is essential for sustainable urban action. And it was this aspect that failed in the restructuring and urban planning project in the Nylon zone in Douala, Cameroon. The World Bank and the SDC had joined forces with the national government to rehabilitate a part of the city at the infrastructural, housing and socio-economic level. Douala had suffered high levels of demographic growth and official neglect; in 1980, the 13 districts of the 'Nylon' zone were home to almost 20 per cent of the city's population: there was no drinkable water, no wastewater processing or garbage disposal system, no asphalt roads, no public schools or health care centres in the area. The project called for the construction of the roads and drainage systems, the installation of collective services, and also the regulation of landownership, housing credits, the relocation of families affected by the works, the promotion of crafts and other types of employment, and support for basic community organisations. This was, in other words, a truly 'integrated' urban project".

The project would never have seen the light of day without civil society and community organisations in these districts. But what happens when such local initiatives are taken over by an international development project? The scope, methods and intervening parties inevitably change. In 1983, the government of Cameroon signed a first agreement with the World Bank for US$55 million of which 36 per cent was lent by the World Bank, 10 per cent by the SDC and the rest by the government. In the end costs skyrocketed, with expenses up by between 50 to 200 per cent.

There was widespread dissatisfaction at the lack of commitment by government authorities, and inhabitants felt excluded by the complexity of institutional structures. Established social practices were marginalised. The residents, mostly migrants of rural origin, had previously organised themselves in order to cope with the most pressing problems prior to the launch of the rehabilitation project, building schools, paths, drains, etc. As the project developed they found themselves progressively eliminated from decision making and relegated to the status of passive onlookers as officials struggled to regulate housing and landownership.

This brief overview of three case studies, highly representative of the problems that confront players in urban agglomerations in developing countries, tells us a lot about the issues that link urban planning and the organisation of a healthy and vibrant urban environment. Without overly simplifying issues that everyone knows to be complex, resolving the problems of planning and organisation requires intervention at three levels:

— The first level is at the level of the neighbourhood, and involves interaction with local authorities, grassroots community organisations, families and individuals. The aim here is to delineate the immediate and more remote problems the residents deal with (gainful employment, schooling for children, housing, sanitation and health) in order to examine their local and wider consequences, possible remedies and their costs.

— The second level is at the district/city level. Urban planners and decision makers need to account for community dynamics and for the changes they bring about in each city area.

— The third level refers to the region surrounding the city, since any change in the city has a direct impact on the hinterland, or even beyond. It is therefore important to know more about the types of interactions that evolve between an urban agglomeration, region, country, and the global world community, in order to make informed political and planning choices for the benefit of the city.

Such a multi-level approach highlights the inconsistencies and contradictions that may occur between social dynamics generated by the inhabitants themselves and decisions made by authorities and implemented in the city. Put side by side, these contradictory choices and political or financial priorities may help redefine urban planning to make it more strategic, flexible and adapted to the existing socio-spatial context – and above all more attentive to the needs and demands of the citizens. Let us review the key elements of sustainable development so as to be able to apply its tenets to urban territories. There are three elements which need to be balanced:

- the environment, which requires judicious and informed management;
- the social sphere, in which an equitable distribution of goods, services and other benefits of economic growth is a key objective; and
- the economy, which will not only aim to be profitable and create material and financial wealth, but will also strive to internalise indirect production costs.

These three key elements of sustainable development, applied to the urban context in developing countries, should be linked to three complementary objectives: territorial planning to avoid an increase of spatial disparities; inclusion of the cultural sphere in order to account for anthropological, historic and symbolic dimensions; and inclusion of the political sphere which provides a regulatory, legal and democratic framework for the changes resulting from the application of sustainable development principles.

Social Services for Sustainable Urban Development

The urbanisation of the world is not a new phenomenon; in fact it is a long-term process that has transformed our societies over the centuries. People congregated in towns and cities, took up increasingly diverse economic activities, and there was a shift from agriculture and husbandry to crafts, trades and industry. Historically speaking, these social and economic changes implied the consolidation of human activities in ever more concentrated human settlements, which facilitated production, trade and other forms of exchange between individuals. Improved communication technology is paving the way for a new spatial distribution of individuals – connected 'virtually', but sometimes physically remote. The city – and its current mutant forms such as urban agglomerations, metropolisation, and metapolisation – was and is at the heart of the restructuring of human societies. The role of urban centres changes throughout history – and also varies according to the continent – but their central position remains. The conditions for their sustainable development cannot be determined uniquely by internal contingencies.

Cities and their inhabitants depend heavily on external resources – energy, natural resources, food, labour. On the other hand, the economic and social activities of their residents generate impacts that go well beyond their spatial and demographic boundaries. Only by analysing the interaction between the city, regional, national and international development will it be possible to design a 'sustainable coherent development strategy'. Existing economic and political relations between the North and the South are characterised by the fact that the use of existing resources, access to services and infrastructures, and consumption of these goods is increasingly inequitable.

On all continents, another socio-spatial division that is becoming increasingly apparent is the primacy of urban centres over rural regions, and – in the urban network – the rising supremacy of very large agglomerations over secondary and intermediate cities. This metropolisation process is evident in the most industrialised countries, and is gathering speed in the developing regions. Limits on financial and human capacities give an unquestionable advantage to metropolitan centres and large agglomerations 'connected' to major national and international networks. This in turn influences political and economic decisions as to public and private investment in planning, collective goods and economic infrastructure.

Urban centres drive economic growth. This is evident in the industrialised countries, but also in Latin America and increasingly in Asia. Scale economies, increased productivity and the concentration of specialised skilled workforces are some of the factors that explain this link between urbanisation and the economy. The latter is highly visible in terms of the estimated contribution of the urban populations to GNP.

The urban primacy in the economic field goes hand in hand with international disparities and more and more precarious urban centres owing to the growth of slums. Intensified trade linkages tend to consolidate this bipolar division of the urban world into 'winners' and 'losers'. Advanced information and communications technologies (ICT) offer economic and political decision makers scope for faster and greater activity; they also give rise to powerful but volatile and unforeseeable migration movements. Weisbrot et al. demonstrate the extent to which deteriorating terms of trade hit the poorest countries hardest. The rift between the rich and the poor has deepened over recent decades and only a few countries have been able to lift themselves out of poverty.

In this context cities are both a 'paradise and a jungle' for their residents and those who aspire to become residents, hoping in their turn to benefit from the accumulation of opportunities that cities embody. As noted earlier, urbanisation will continue on a global scale for the foreseeable future. In 2007, the world's urban population will equal its rural population; in 2030, it will represent 60.2 per cent of the overall population of our planet, that is, almost five billion people, four billion of these in developing countries, out of a total world population of 8.27 billion.

The combined dynamics of demographic growth, urbanisation, trade globalisation and the spread of advanced technologies, deregulation and increasingly precarious social conditions all combine to create the impression that in developing countries urban areas will continue to grow in a dual discriminatory fashion: territorial fragmentation, with increasingly limited areas of prosperity and wellbeing surrounded by areas of social exclusion. This process will be marked by increasingly informal relationships, particularly in the economic sphere, giving rise to individual and social insecurity. Against such a backdrop, the slogan launched by the UN in its Human Settlements Program of 'cities without slums' appears to be based more on an act of faith than on analysis. From a critical perspective, then, progress needs to be made on four different fronts:

— The most important priority appears to be the creation of a concerted policy to combat slums in a fundamentally structured manner, backed by political authorities on all levels and designed over the long term. Overcoming disparities and social inequity calls for the mobilisation and involvement of all stakeholders, particularly the participation of inhabitants and their representatives. It is possible to detect a certain 'political indifference' towards the major issues of urbanisation in the developing countries. Instead of expecting inhabitants, especially the poorest ones, to adapt to ad hoc bureaucratic and administrative practices that encourage social exclusion and clientelism, an alternative approach is needed to rebuild urban and national legal and regulatory frameworks adapted to the population's needs and capable of responding to sectoral demands.

— There is a need to challenge the neo-liberal bias in structural adjustment programs that disempowers public authorities and disadvantaged urban populations by making the economies of Third World countries increasingly 'informal'. Going beyond such basic considerations as employment and income generation, poverty reduction and access to basic goods, the urban economy should be redesigned as a driving force of development that is both socially and environmentally acceptable. It needs to be innovative in its use of technologies, and act in a way so as to redress territorial imbalance.

— Due to the combination of a lack of access to credit and precarious personal circumstances, many urban households are forced to seek alternative forms of credit which are socially and financially burdensome (e.g. usury, pawnbroking, mafia sources). This inadequacy of the banking system to serve clients who are numerous but have low income generates very heavy indirect costs for the whole of society by encouraging illegal landownership and construction, the spread of anarchic patterns of land use, and the use of low-quality building materials. Alternative solutions for the construction and financing of subsidised housing for the poor do exist. These have been tested in various cities in the world; they all revolve around a few key innovations: micro-credits, family and community guarantees. Like the other institutional change described above, they aim to adapt the financial system to the needs of the inhabitants rather than the other way around.

If policy was reorientated in this way, it could truly contribute to tackling the main urban dysfunctions observed earlier, and help fulfill the Millennium

Development Agenda: to contribute to the eradication of extreme poverty and hunger by reducing the proportion of people whose income is less than US$1 per day by half by 2015; by reducing the number of people without access to healthy drinking water by 50 per cent by 2015; and to significantly improving living conditions for at least 100 million slum dwellers by 2020.

5

Urban Healthcare Services

Urban poor population constitutes nearly a third of India's urban population and is growing at three times the national population growth rate. Health status and access of reproductive and child health services of slum dwellers is poor and comparable to the rural population. Public sector urban health delivery system, especially for poor, has so far been sporadic, far from adequate and limited in its reach. Other factors contributing to inadequate reach of services are illegality, social exclusion of slums, hidden slum pockets, weak social fabric, lacking coordination among various stakeholders and neglected political consciousness.

Opportunities for impacting urban health are several. Efforts to improve the conditions of urban poor necessitate strengthening national policy and fiscal mandate, augmenting and strengthening the urban health delivery system, coordinating among multiple stakeholders, involving private sector, strengthening municipal functioning and building community capacities. Public Health Initiatives for more than India's 1 billion people are aimed at mitigating disease burden and improving health. These endeavors have been on for the past several decades. A few notable of these include Universal Immunisation Progamme, Child Survival and

Safe Motherhood Program, Reproductive Child Health Program, and Integrated Child Development Scheme.

The National Rural Health Mission (NRHM) represents a renewal, convergence and heightening of attention to disease prevention, communicable disease control, health protection and promotion. NRHM approach reflects the growing realisation among public health professionals that continued investment in clinical care brings diminishing returnsand that aliments and problems addressed so successfully by public health measures in several countries and among the better off segments of India's population still persist among a very large proportion of our population. The NHRM provides an opportunity for health administrators to

a) provide need-based health care
b) ensure reach of public health services to the underserved segments through vitalised health system
c) enable socio-economically and educationally weak communities to take better care of their health and
d) bring all pieces of the health and intricately linked sectors to function in a harmonised and complementary manner to optimise impact.

While public health indicators in India had improved measurably over the last few decades, a plateauing has been observed during the last 10 years. Among several factors contributing to this plateau a notable issue is that the essential public health services have remained inaccessible for large segments of India's population in rural as well as in urban areas.

Urbanisation of Poverty

Urban growth has been exponential in India over the last few decades. While India's rural population has doubled from 1961-2001 the urban population has grown four fold. Out of the total population of 1027 million as on 1st March, 2001, 742 million lived in rural areas and 285 million in urbanareas. The percentage decadal growth of population in rural and urban areas during the decade was 17.9 and 31.2 percent respectively.

Population projections by the United Nations indicate that by 2030, India's urban population will grow to 576 million and constitute 40 per cent of the total population. In 2001, there were 35 cities with million plus population and 393 cities above 100,000 population. It is estimated that the number of million plus cities in India will grow to 51 by 2011 and 75 by 2021. In addition there would be 500 large cities with population above 100,000 by 2021.The Indian demographic scenario represents a 2-3-4-5 syndrome: in the last decade, as India grew at an average annual growth rate of 2%, urban India grew at 3%, mega cities at 4% and slum populations rose by 5-6%.

Estimates of poverty ratio in urban areas range from 67 millionto 90 million. However, these estimates do not reflect the true magnitude of urban poverty because of "un-accounted" for, unrecognised squatter settlements and other populations residing on pavements, construction sites, fringes etc. Large Urban slum and other urban poor populations have remained unreached by the public health services.

Poverty is not merely a rural phenomenon. As a proportion of total poverty, the urban component has increased from 15% in the early 1970s to about 25% in the mid 1990s.In other words; one out of four poor persons of the country is now an urban resident.

The rapid growth of slum population is contributed by:

a) Migration into a city from villages and smaller towns owing to better employment opportunities, diminution of rural agricultural land and related livelihood opportunities;

b) Natural increase in urban poor population which has a higher fertility rate than urban middle and upper class;

c) Expansion of city boundaries to include peripheral rural areas, some of which get converted into slums as erstwhile rural land is colonised for housing purposes.

Status of Urban Health

Slum dwellers in cities suffer from adverse health conditions owing to insufficient services, low awareness, and poor environment. However, the rhetoric of urban bias in development and better conditions in urban areas vis-à-vis rural areas has masked the real picture of urban poor. Millennium Development Goal 7 (Target 11) aims to significantly improve the lives of at least 100 million slum dwellers world wide by the year 2020. Even this very conservative target seems a tall order unless this large underserved section of population is adequately reached through public health services.

Child, infant and neonatal survival among urban poor is similar to rural population. Under-5, infant and neonatal mortality rates are considerably higher among urban poor as compared to urban averagesand almost as worse as their rural counterparts.

More than half of India's urban poor children are underweight. In most States, undernutrition among urban poor children is worse than in rural areas. Survival patterns among the urban poor, clearly point at the need for extra focus on this large segment of India's population.

The reach of essential preventive health services to the urban poor and utilisation of health services by these segments is abysmally low: a) about 60% of children are not completely immunised by 1 year of age; b) use of birth spacing methods is abjectly low at 4%; c) almost 6 out of 10 babies are delivered at home in the absence of a trained health worker.The meager access of MCH services among urban poor is obscured by urban averages.

Access to Health Services

The eight large and less developed EAG States of India constitute 32% of India's urban population and are home to 28 million urban poor . In these less developed states under-5 mortality and Infant mortality among the urban poor is about 1.3 times and 1.6 times higher than their respective National figures. Access to RCH services amongst urban poor is also worse than other states of the country.

- Institutional deliveries, among urban poor in UP are 6.5 times lesser (13.1%) than in Tamil Nadu (85.6%).
- Similarly, complete immunisation coverage among urban poor in UP is 29.7 percent compared to 74.4 in Tamil Nadu. Poorer access to services has contributed largely to deprived health conditions of urban poor in these states.

Government Efforts to Improve Urban Health

Though Government efforts have been primarily rural centric, a few urban schemes have been implemented in the past. These include the Urban Family Welfare Scheme, Urban Revamping Scheme, Sterilisation bed scheme and post partum centers in urban areas. However, the coverage of the schemes has been far from complete. The rapid growth in urban population has further eroded the coverage levels of these schemes. Recently, the World Bank funded India Population

Projects have attempted to provide health care services the urban poor. However, these schemes have been operational only in the mega cities like Delhi, Mumbai and Chennai.

Factors Affecting the Effectiveness of Health Services

Those with the greatest need for health care often have least access to it. Reach and effectiveness of maternal and child health services in urban slums are strained by several challenges. These can be classified into the four categories viz., Systemic Factors, Urban Poor Related Factors, Weak Coordination among and limited capacity of Stakeholders, and Inadequate Political and Civil Society Consciousness.

Systemic Factors

The existing Urban Health Delivery System is far from adequate to respond to needs of escalating urban poor population.

1. *Lack of organised public sector infrastructure and services in urban areas:* Despite accounting for one-fourth of the country's poor population, urban areas have less than 4%of Govt. Primary Health Care facilities. With a total urban population of 285 million, the available Urban Primary Health Infrastructure translates to one health facility (UFWC/HP) for about 1.5 lakh urban population. IPP-VIII and other programs operational only in selected cities did not reach all urban poor even in these cities. Large number of urban areas have been completely left out or poorly targeted. Health Posts were established in only 10 States of the country. 32% of health posts were established in Maharashtra while the scheme remained uninitiated in Bihar. Only about $1/10^{th}$ of the sterilisation beds are in EAG states .Staffing has also not increased in response to urban growth.

2. *Higher allocation for Bigger Cities:* There is inequitable distribution of available resources for urban poor among different cities. While, medium–small cities have significant urban population most urban programs have focused on mega cities like Mumbai, Delhi, Kolkata, Chennai. These mega cities are preferred to other relatively smaller cities for financing since they have greater management and negotiation capacity that enables them to garner more resources. It is projected that many of the presently smaller cities will join the rank of million-plus cities in the next two decades. Thus preparedness in the smaller cities is needed to meet this growing challenge.

3. *Poor access and utilisation despite proximity:* Poor access despite proximity is a result of a) weak demand b) minimal outreach services c) very weak community-provider linkages d) timings that often do not suit the daily wage earning urban poor. Urban poor prefer home deliveries despite availability of government and private hospitals, because of concerns like, securer environment at home, nobody to take care of other siblings at home in event of hospitalisation, perceived unfriendly treatment at Government hospitals, and expensive private health care facilities. Poor access of services is also reflective of the family having to cope with imperative issues such the risk of eviction and struggle for access to basic services like water and sanitation, all these being compounded by low health awareness.

4. *Lack of sensitisation among the service providers:* Sense of apathy towards slum dwellers, considered an 'unnecessary intrusion' into the city, exists among service providers. Health service provides are often

rough in their behavior towards slum dwellers. This dissuades the latter from availing services.

5. *Poor living environment that compounds the lack of health services:* This rapid, unplanned urbanisation and simultaneous growth of urban population in limited urban living spaces visibly impacts the quality of life of slum dwellers. Access to water supply and sanitation facilities among the urban poor is low. 61.7% of urban poor households do not receive piped water supply and 65.9% do not have any toilet facility.

When infrastructure and services are lacking, urban settlements are amongst the world's most life threatening environments. Child mortality and morbidity (diarrhea in particular) have been associated with poor water quantity and quality, lack of sanitation and poor hygiene practices. Location of slums in unhygienic surroundings accentuates health adversity. Slums located adjacent to large open drains have a greater incidence of diarrhea and other water-borne diseases .Slums adjacent to waste disposal sites face hazards of polluted water and air. Pigs, vultures and other animals affect levels of hygiene maintainable in a slum thereby increasing the risk of spread of infection amongst children who come in close contact with the outside environment.

Urban Poor Related Factors

Issues pertaining to 'urban poor' populations also pose further challenges in urban health care.

1. *Illegality of slums and Social Exclusion:* Slums are almost always initially informal settlements with no land tenure rights. They are considered synonymous with pockets of dirty, diseased and gloomy people and wished to disappear to make way for a clean and posh neighborhood by their upper and middle

class neighbors. Governments often try to relocate and at some other times demolish entire slums to 'clean up the city' or for meeting legal obligations. The demolition drive that left 4.5 lakh people homeless was part of Vision 2020, the government's plan to make Mumbai a "world-class" city like Shanghai. Planners and service providers often harbor the perspective that providing service to 'illegal slums' implies giving them legal sanctity. In Indore, immunisation services scarcely reached nonnotified slums while notified slums received benefits of repeated interventions.

2. *Large proportions of slums are invisible:* Services usually do not reach hidden and missing pockets of urban poverty that are not part of official slum lists such as limestone and brick-kiln workers, construction site workers, workers of local industry (leather, jute, glass). Bound to a specific industry, they are usually on some private land, unseen by most. Owing to long delays in updating of official slum list in most cities, slums may remain unrecognised for years. As an example, in Agra city, as per the list of Department of Urban Development Authority (DUDA), there were 215 slums with an estimated population of 3 lakh. An assessment of the underserved population, conducted in 2005 for planning Agra's Urban Health Project, identified 393 slums with a population of approximately 8 lakh.

3. *Weak social fabric, collective negotiation capacity:* Issues like illegality, social exclusion, uncertainty of land tenure, threat of eviction, and being forced to live in a disabling environment result in a sense of resignation among slum dwellers about their surroundings and wellbeing with compromised motivation to invest in infrastructure.

Other factors like heterogeneity among slum dwellers due to in-migration from different areas, varied cultures, fewer extended family connections, and more women engaged in work leads to lesser willingness and fewer occasions to build urban slum community as a strong collective unit.

4. *Temporary Migration and Floating Populations:* Temporary migration to their native villages, especially of pregnant women for delivery results in missing out receiving services from either residence. Mother and baby do not receive services in the village due to distances, unavailability of previous record of services received and lack of awareness and negotiating capacity. Health service delivery for floating population in urban areas is a challenge for urban health planners. Large cities and religious towns have substantial and regular inflow of floating population. Mumbai city officials estimate about 2-3 million floating population. City population of Haridwar, a religious town, is virtually overrun by pilgrims on special occasions in the year particularly the Magh Mela, Baisakhi, Kanwar Mela. Pilgrims run into tens of millions, once every 6 years during Kumbh / Ardh Kumbh

Weak Coordination among Stakeholders

There are multiple urban health stakeholders including Health and Family Welfare Department, ICDS, ULBs, DUDA, NGOs, CBOs, Donor Agencies, Professional Bodies (IMA, IAP), Formal and informal Private practitioners, Corporate sector, Charitable Organisations, Employee State Insurance and local resources such as schools. These stakeholders operate in isolation with little coordination. They can benefit greatly by sharing resources, information, and expertise and avoiding duplication of efforts.

The capacity of ULBs except in larger metropolitan cities is observed to be weak. In most of the 73rd rapidly urbanising 2 lakh to 40 lakh size cities, Maternal and Child Health service delivery capacity of Municipal bodies is grossly inadequate. Most Municipal Bodies have insufficient health program management experience which is also responsible for the underutilisation of funds available under various Central government schemes such as the National Slum Development Programme (NSDP).

Inadequate Political and Civil Society Consciousness

Major political forces appear to harbor a significant greater rural bias while thinking of poverty. This has resulted in most attention being paid to rural poverty while the poor in urban areas have been neglected or at best provided passing reference in government policies and programmes. An analysis of rural and urban ICDS coverage shows that one AWC to total population ratio in rural areas is 1:1260 and 1:6114 in urban areas. The civil society also views slums with indifference.

SOCIAL WORK IN URBAN HEALTH SECTOR

Though the challenges in improving the health of the urban poor are many, there are several opportunities which can be leveraged to reach the objective of better health in urban slums. These include:

— *Growing Recognition of the problem and burgeoning interest:* The Government has acknowledged non-availability as well as substantial under utilisation of available primary health care facilities in urban areas along with an overcrowding at secondary and tertiary care centers. MCH services to urban poor have been recognised as important thrust area by the government under the National Population

Policy-2000, National Health Policy-2002, Draft RCH II and the Tenth Five Year Plan. The MOHFW has constituted a "Task Force to advise the NRHM on "Strategies for Urban Health Care" which indicates the Government's commitment to improve health services for the urban poor.

— *Resources and Potential Partners Abound:* City planners and programmers can collaborate with a range of public sector and private partners: Health Dept., NGOs, Private and Charitable hospitals, ULBs amongst other to have a greater impact on health services coverage in urban slums.

— *Urban Poor Geographically Approachable:* Crowded living of slums and their proximity to the already existing government and private health services makes larger number of people geographically accessible for outreach activities in lesser time unlike rural areas where population is more dispersed.

— *74th Constitutional Amendment, an Opportunity for City Governments:* The 74th Constitutional Amendment which delegates powers and responsibilities to ULBs is a big opportunity to improve the conditions in disadvantaged urban settlements. Under the 12Schedule of the 74Amendment, health services are mandated as functions of ULBs. It is also in the political interest of elected representatives to utilise this opportunity and broaden the spectrum of their current activities to include health services to the urban poor. This will help better serve and nurture their constituencies.

— *Basic Health issues are those with which we are familiar:* Technical health priorities of antenatal care, safe / clean deliveries, neonatal care, immunisation, diarrhea and ARI are all issues that public health programmers are familiar with. Interventions for the above priorities e.g. diarrhea prevention and treatment or malnutrition prevention are well established.

— *Urban poor can be easily reached for communication activity:* Exposure to mass media has been shown to have substantial effects on people's attitudes and behaviors in India, even after controlling for urban / rural residence.Since availability and access of mass media is higher in urban areas, urban poor can be easily reached for communication activity and are more likely to embrace change.

Some approaches to improve health of the Urban Poor as we move forward on the agenda of progressing towards achieving aims of the National Rural Health Mission are given below.

— *Strengthen National Policy, Fiscal Mandate and Vitalise Implementation:* It will be crucial to ensure an equitable rural-urban distribution when allocating resources for policies and programs aimed at improving health of the population. Existing policies need to be improved to make them more urban poor friendly, practical and measurable. Broadening the scope and focus of the National Rural Health Mission to unequivocally include the urban poor and re-designating it as the National Public Health Mission merits consideration. Energetic policy implementation can be ensured through a) regular training of officers and b) increasing information about various schemes to urban poor. Civil Society uproar generated from time to time will add the very helpful social push. Measures for ensuring implementation of 74th constitutional amendment and strengthening ULBs are needed.

— *Strengthen and Augment Urban Health Delivery System:* Once the NRHM focus is expanded to include health services to the urban poor, an operational plan for strengthening urban health services will have to be put in place. There is a clear need to a) develop, support and strengthen dedicated Public Sector Infrastructure for urban health services with special focus on preventive services for slum dwellers and b) establish Urban Health Authority at City and State levels within the institutional framework of NRHM with clear roles, responsibilities and accountability for result based indices of the urban-poor. To improve reach and quality of health services there is a need to a) provide motivational training to health providers (ANMs, MOs, Supervisors) to be more sensitive towards the disadvantaged and to coordinate effectively with slum based Community Health Volunteers (along the line of the Accredited Social health activist proposed for rural areas in NRHM) and with slum level CBOs; b) develop a delivery system that is responsive to the needs of slum dwellers and facilitates them to avail services; c) regularise outreach services in slums; d) Provide health card to every urban child to ensure basic health services.

— *Go beyond Notified slums to find the Urban Poor:* The urban health component of NRHM would need to define approach to developing city level urban health plans which are responsive to the urban context. Comprehensive planning is critical to ensure that un-listed and invisible urban poor clusters or slums (which are also the neediest) are reached. Official slum lists need be regularly updated. Public health service administrators need to be sensitised that legality / notification related issues do not come in the way of reaching out to a family or a cluster with basic health services as mandated in the Indian constitution. Since urban poor populations are highly mobile and diverse an in-built flexibility will enable urban health services ensure that such population are included.

— *Coordinate among Multiple Stakeholders:* The NRHM has mandated convergence of different sectors for optimal utilisation of available resources. This aspect of the NRHM assumes greater relevance in urban areas where presence of many stakeholders is a palpable opportunity. For enhancing reach to the urban poor it is important to utilise resources from different departments / sectors. For example regular coordination meetings between various stakeholders at ward level in Indore facilitated by a non-governmental organisation have resulted in improved health services to the low income populations. Health department could collaborate with other stakeholders (water and sanitation departments) and NGOs to provide basic environmental improvements and health services in slums. The inter-sectoral convergence approaches being developed for NRHM could be expanded and adapted to include urban specific sectors and stakeholders to improve health services for the urban poor.

— *Involve Private Sector:* NRHM has clearly identified Public Private Partnerships as a key approach towards vitalising implementation of health programs and mandated a significant role for NGOs. In urban areas, involving (private doctors, charitable facilities, NGOs, Corporate sector) for defined essential services including outreach services is a clear opportunity. Public Private Partnership (PPP) can be an important bridge strategy for meeting the public health challenge of quickly expanding services and reaching to the under-served. Slums uncovered by health services were covered by PPP in Andhra Pradesh, Bangalore and Guwhati. PPP enables use of existing Public and Private infrastructure and capacities to expand services rather than invest time in building new infrastructure-saving costs and time.

— *Strengthen Municipal Functioning:* To pursue the mandate enshrined in the 12schedule of the 74Constitutional Amendment, it is essential that municipalities are equipped adequately for urban health programming, generating resources at the local level, better financial management and effectively engaging with private sector partners. Extra focus on EAG States: NRHM has identified certain high focus States where there is a greater need for improving health services. From within NRHM high focus states, the low performing EAG States, which are home to 43% of India's urban poor, present a special challenge of poorer health status and poor availability of services for urban disadvantaged. Program planning, implementation and monitoring capacity is far weaker than the better performing states. Municipal governance and program and fiscal capacity is also weaker than other states. These EAG States also present a special opportunity being a small number of administrative units which have the potential to vastly expand and improve urban health services with support and encouragement. Greater emphasis through capacity enhancement efforts, more frequent review and hand holding to these states will enable them reach out to a very large proportion of the country's urban poor. Pilot lead programs could be established in one or two cities in each of EAG States to serve as early learning sites as an impetus to further urban health efforts and as an impetus to advance urban health efforts.

— *Build Capacity of Slum Communities for Improved Utilisation of Services:* The NRHM outlines the need to strengthen community level capacities to improve health of the communities and the need to measure outcomes at the community level. To address low uptake of services by urban poor it is vital to a) strengthen community-provider linkages through a trained cadre of slum based health volunteers similar to the ASHA proposed in NRHM, women health groups and other appropriate strategies b) build capacity of community groups to facilitate promotion of context relevant behaviors pertaining to maternal and child health. NGOs can play a crucial role by building capacity of slum communities and thus enhance utilisation of public sector services.

6

Social Work in Modern Urban Society

In recent years, governments have imposed and refined systems of audit and new operational and administrative procedures. Social work practice has become more legalised, and notions of 'evidence-based practice' have become pervasive. These developments, which emphasise practitioner accountability to stakeholders other than clients, seem to dominate the nature of what it is to be a practitioner, particularly in the public sector. As Stepney has argued, there seems little doubt that practitioners experience these initiatives as increasing managerial control. Moreover, the emphasis on technical recording, systematic information gathering, performance indicators, all tend to reinforce mechanistic practice rather than creativity and innovation'. Social workers are required to take a more instrumental and impersonal approach to their work, and perceive that care for service users is little more than labour in the service of economy, efficiency, and effectiveness.

Recent years have also witnessed the publication of a number of texts which have attempted to develop perspectives which are explicitly critical and reflexive and which, to varying degrees, draw upon insights offered by a number of postmodern perspectives. Peter Leonard characterises these developments as 'reconstructing the emancipatory project'. Partly drawing on

Leonard, Jan Fook and Karen Healy see the essential elements of these emerging critical social work approaches as emphasising a: commitment to standing alongside oppressed and impoverished populations; the importance of dialogic relations between workers and service users; the significance of social, economic, and political systems in shaping individual experiences and social relationships, including interactions within the practice context; an orientation towards the transformation of processes and structures that perpetuate domination and exploitation, and thus emphasises the importance of social justice and equality. Significantly for our purposes, Healy notes that proponents of critical social work have 'persistently challenged the occupational self image of social work as a caring profession by emphasizing the complicity of social workers in the reproduction of the oppressive conditions within the practice context and beyond it'.

In many respects the modernisation agenda can be seen as a reaction against the inflexibility, inefficiency and aloofness of both large stage bureaucracies and the professionals who play key roles in the delivery of services. The changes introduced are seen as making a serious attempt to improve collaboration, inclusiveness and transparency, by a much greater emphasis on involving citizens in decision-making at both a local strategic level and in individual cases. The visions for the future are articulated in the language of community and citizenship, reciprocity and responsibility, justice and fairness, partnership and participation, and crucially recognise that a variety of state, voluntary and informal services provide vital contributions to the care and support of individuals and thus the health of society more generally. At the same time the way in which such changes have been introduced has very much been of a top-down nature. More particularly, the process of modernisation can be seen as furthering the growing managerialisation of social work and social care via its intense focus on performance and efficiency targets, together with the growing emphasis of centralised and formulaic regimes of inspection and scrutiny. Thus while many of the more liberatory and radical elements of social work theory and practice can be seen, at one level, to have received official endorsement and to have entered the mainstream, at another level they can be seen to have been transformed into a variety of mechanisms for the increased regulation of both social workers and the people with whom they work.

Discussions of care within the critical social work literature, until very recently, have been remarkable only by their absence, such that it has seemed there has almost been an assumption that social work is so tainted by its associations with care that the word should be expunged both from its lexicon and rationale. In our view this is unfortunate. Not only has the notion of care been at the core of social work values, theory and practice since its inception but it is the central part of our argument that its rehabilitation can provide a key counterweight to the increasing processes of managerialisation which seem so pervasive.

Further, however, we argue that the dominance of the managerialist discourse has deleterious effects on attempts to modernise social work and social care. Unless care is relocated at the centre of debates, policies and practices, the elements which can be seen to make social work and social care more generally distinctive will be lost. That social work practitioners value care, and perceive that their desire to prioritise it in their practice is not shared by government funders is illustrated for us in a recent study comparing practitioners' perceptions of their own and their funding department's priorities in non-government family support services. Experienced family support practitioners were offered a list of eight characteristics from which to choose those they considered to be the three most important characteristics of effective services. The characteristics included client, legal, management, and worker orientations. Practitioners ranked first the client-oriented characteristic that 'the service enables clients to achieve their goals', with 80 per cent of those surveyed including this criterion in their top three. Practitioners perceived that the funding department's top priority was the legally oriented characteristic that 'the service complies with legal obligations, such as child protection legislation', with 91 per cent of practitioners including this in their list of the department's top three. Whereas 44 per cent of practitioners included the characteristic 'workers are compassionate and caring' among their top three, only five per cent perceived it to be a priority for the Department.

Other studies aiming to imagine the ideal organisational context for caring work emphasise how professional and other caregivers need room to exercise both their judgement and their emotional commitment to those they care for. That service users highly value care is confirmed in numerous studies over the years demonstrating the importance of the relationship and the caring approach of the worker to service user experience of social service quality . At the same time, we are aware that the early years of the new millennium have witnessed the publication of a number of texts which have underlined the importance for social work and social care of seriously engaging with feminist thinking about the 'ethics of care'. Such developments provide us with a real possibility for not just rehabilitating the notion of care to the centre of social work but in a way which contributes to and builds on the arguments developed within the critical social work literature.

More particularly it seems to use that the epistemological arguments within the discourse of the ethics of care, together with its more 'politicised' conceptions, can provide an important resource whereby social work can engage with the modernisation agenda. Of particular importance is the capacity of the discourse of the ethics of care to offer ways of conceiving and representing those aspects of social work which are obscured by the rational technical focus of the managerialism that has come to dominate the way social work and social care is increasingly thought about, organised and practised.

Rationalisation of Social Work

While religious convictions about the nature of human struggles shaped social work during its development in the latter part of the nineteenth century, the twentieth century saw increasing attempts to professionalise the role. The main protagonists aspired to mimic the traditional professions, particularly medicine, but at no time has social work achieved this level of authority, status or legitimacy. Rather, although its organisation differs internationally, the development of social work during much of the twentieth century is better characterised as a 'bureau-profession'; certainly bureaucratisation as much as professionalisation has shaped its development, particularly in the state sectors.

As models of organisation, decision-making, and practice, professionalism and bureaucracy, have shaped social workers' capacity to enact care. One way of seeing the 'problem' these approaches pose for the theory and practice of social work is to look through the lens of gender. If we see masculinity and femininity not as attributes of individuals in any essentialist sense but as cultural representations, it is possible to explore the gendering of social institutions in a way that makes some of the dilemmas of caring, and in particular the ambiguities and paradoxes of professional care, much more explicit.

As a normative cultural project, masculinity entails separation from others, the creation of a strongly bounded sense of self, an emphasis on individuality, a wish for power, agency and action, and for being a subject—making a difference in the world; whereas femininity involves a continuing experience of connection with others, a focus on interdependence, and a sense of self in relation to others, rather than as always autonomous and apart. Masculinity is crucially concerned with establishing relations of domination and ensuring their stability and predictability. The public world created by men with its visions of rational action and appropriate rules of behaviour, corresponds directly to this. Autonomous, controlled individuals are brought into ordinary relations with each other in pursuit of agreed goals. Emotions, enthusiasms, and vulnerabilities are seen to be an impediment. It is not, however, that they have been done away with but they have been confined to the private sphere that is seen as primarily dominated by women.

In its ideal typical form, the bureaucratic approach emphasises formality and distance as the only routes to rational decision making. The impartiality of the decision, the impersonality of the bureaucrat, and the unequivocal authority of its hierarchy are the key characteristics of bureaucracy. It is not difficult to see that the ideal typical bureaucracy is a masculine, not a neutral institutional type as its advocates assume. Masculinity's version of rational action conceives itself as autonomous and independent of the other. The impartiality, impersonality, formality, and distance characterising the ideal typical bureaucracy reflect these masculine cultural characteristics. Bureaucratisation is the attempt to enact a normative framework which prioritises the atomistic, autonomous, self-contained individual, thereby marginalising the relational and contextual nature of the work carried out within the organisation. In apparent contrast, the ideal typical professional appears to have all of the flexibility that the rule and hierarchy bound bureaucrat lacks.

The true professional acts autonomously, refers difficult cases to a more experienced colleague, and is not required to bow to hierarchy as the bureaucrat would be. However, as Celia Davies has argued, while bureaucratic and professional approaches may seem at first sight diametrically opposed, on closer inspection the notion of the professional is similarly gendered masculine.

The ideal typical professional is detached, treats each patient or client with a correct professional concern, and is not bound up with their crises or their pain. Again, there is a strong element of the need for distance and impersonality. Expertise derives from formal training, which is itself based on rational science. Perhaps most crucially, autonomy stands at the very heart of traditional concepts of the professional.

In many respects, therefore, and as Davies argues, the ideal types of the professional and the bureaucratic forms of practice and organisation share much. Both are oriented to control and mastery; to establish order through implementation of an abstract decision set of processes. Both rely on hierarchical relations and promote distance from their clienteles.

The application of expert knowledge, whether associated with the office of the bureaucrat or the person of the professional, retains a mysterious character and calls forth deference on the part of the client. Both the bureaucrat and the professional are invested with an authority for decision making as if they inhabit a sovereign court, where their decisions are rarely questioned, and where those on the receiving end are grateful.

Social work has never had this kind and level of authority and power. The designation 'bureau-profession' is simply one sign of its failure to achieve full professional status. More particularly, the nature of social work, particularly its engagement with the most marginalised and deprived members of society, meant that it had difficulty in fulfilling the characteristics required to fulfil this status. Traditionally, social work has emphasised the importance of the worker-client relationship, rarely falling back on a narrowly defined, autonomous approach to its operations.

It is not a coincidence that social work—a predominantly female occupation—has traditionally emphasised the relational and caring aspects of its work, characteristics that do not lend themselves easily to either the professional or the bureaucratic models. More recent years have seen an important shift in its trajectory of development.

The alleged failures and problems of social work that became apparent in a series of child abuse tragedies and public inquiries during the 1970s and 1980s prefigured the increasing criticisms of most health and welfare professional occupations that emerged in the political and public arenas during the 1990s. Both the bureaucratic and professional approaches to health and welfare which became so dominant in the post-war period were seen to be wanting. Simultaneously, there occurred increasing questioning of the welfare state and the growth of a new approach to health and welfare which placed the notion of managerialism at its centre.

This context of failure has provided the key ideological impetus for criticising and trying to move beyond the models of both the bureaucracy and the profession which were central to the way health and welfare services were thought about and organised in the second half of the twentieth century. Governments have sought to remedy this failure with a new governance model: managerialism, often referred to as the 'new public management'. While the thrust and emphases of policy differ under different political regimes, managerialism has risen to dominance in most advanced liberal societies in the Western world, particularly North America, the United Kingdom, and Australia in recent years.

From the managerialist perspective, professionals and bureaucrats are self interested and untrustworthy. Both need to be 'managed' by new mechanisms that establish clear lines and criteria of accountability, to restore the integrity of and community trust in public services. Amongst other innovations, managerialist governments have developed and implemented a variety of practices designed to monitor, assess, and regulate the performance of both organisations and workers delivering public services, and those in receipt of them. These practices and their supporting ideas aim to promote a costconscious performance culture. Concepts—and often practices—of competition between providers and choice for customers have proliferated, as if service provision occurred in a quasi-market.

Proponents claim that these innovations remedy the problems of the old bureaucratic or professionalised approaches. However, importantly for our argument, the social relations managerialism represents and aims to institutionalise have many of the masculine characteristics already discussed. Like the bureaucrat and the professional, the ideal new manager remains distant and controlled. He takes a critical stance towards the arguments presented and the established practices of others, drawing his own conclusions based on designated general decision rules, rather than being swayed by sympathy to particular cases. Managerialism seems to celebrate critique, distance, and the ability to make difficult decisions, such that there is no attempt to hide potential hostility and warring in the way professional and bureaucratic approaches might have.

The cultural codes of masculinity seem even more explicit and are celebrated in a much more obvious way in a climate which is seen as driven by concerns about risk, increased globalisation, and the recognition that no one can be seen to fall back on traditional notions of authority. In this context debates about the ethics of care can provide a vital critical framework for not just understanding some key elements of the current contexts and realities of day-today practice, but also for helping us move beyond them.

Theory and Practice of Critical Social Work

In the early 1980s, feminist philosophers and political theorists began to overcome their historical uneasiness about engaging in debates about morality and ethics, to develop an explicitly gender-sensitive approach to moral inquiry. Perhaps the most significant product of feminism's engagement with moral philosophy has been the discourse of the ethics of care. In the ensuing twenty years, debate about the ethics of care has itself burgeoned. Our purpose here is not to provide a detailed exposition of the evolution of the discourse of the ethics of care or to account for the emergence of different strands. Rather, we aim to set out the shared assumptions and characteristic ways of thinking of proponents of the ethics of care, and to highlight some points of contention of particular importance to assessing the usefulness of the ethics of care for the theory and practice of critical social work, and to demonstrate its potential for providing both a counterweight to the managerialist dominance to current attempts to 'modernise' social work and social care in England and elsewhere.

The shared assumptions of the ethics of care are a set of interwoven arguments about the nature of the good in human interactions, and of how moral subjects generate and act on knowledge about the good.

First among these shared assumptions of care ethics is what Selma Sevenhuijsen calls a 'relational ontology': the ethics of care places at the centre of moral inquiry the interdependence of humans and their responsibilities to each other, rather than individuals and their rights.

Second, the ethics of care recognises the equal moral worth of all persons, and holds that their informal and interpersonal relations are an appropriate object and ground of moral deliberation.

Third, the ethics of care emphasises caring as moral posture or disposition: moral subjects should attend to others with compassion, responding to each person as unique and irreplaceable, and recognising each moral decision as taking place within a specific context. This contrasts with conventional rights-based ethics, in which the aim is to 'rise above' personal attachment, to consider right action from the standpoint of a disinterested and disengaged moral actor.

Fourth, the nurturing at the heart of care ethics requires that caring is also a process that fosters the growth of those participating in caring relationships, and their willingness to take on open-ended responsibilities in regard to each other. From the perspective of care ethics, certain emotions, particularly empathy and compassion, are not fetters on clear and objective moral judgement, but rather are fundamental to the development of moral understanding itself. Moreover, if a moral subject is to attend to another in their concrete specificity—that is to say, to take into account both the uniqueness of the person, and the complex details of their life situation—moral decision-making will require much more than the application of principles. Feelings, the capacity to recognise 'the separate consciousness of another making its own sense of the world', and communication are all required. This adds up to what Margaret Walker calls: an alternative moral epistemology, a very different way of identifying and appreciating the forms of intelligence which define responsible moral action. This view does not imagine our moral understandings congealed into a compact theoretical instrument of impersonal decision for each person, but as deployed in shared processes of discovery, expression, interpretation, and adjustment between persons'.

Although theorists of the ethics of care agree on these matters of substance and method in moral reasoning, there remain several significant, well-recognised, and related points of contention. These include the way the role of gender, particularly femininity, is conceptualised in different strands of care ethics, the relationship between the ethics of care and traditional justice or rights-based ethical theories, and the extent to which a framework for moral reasoning modelled on personal relationships can address broader social problems of injustice and oppression. It is worth exploring different views on these issues among theorists of care ethics, because different constructions of these aspects of care ethics pose different opportunities and risks for social work.

Some theorists of care ethics such as Nel Noddings construct an avowedly 'feminine' ethic of care in explicit opposition to rights-based ethics. Noddings, Sara Ruddick, Virginia Held, and other influential early contributors to the discourse of the ethics of care were motivated to counter the at best patronising, at worst entirely dismissive way women and the feminine had been treated in conventional ethical inquiry. These thinkers relied heavily on the mother-child relationship as a model for thinking through an alternative model of moral reasoning, placing personal relationships in the private domain at the centre. Nel Noddings, for example, in a web of arguments about gender, human nature, and moral obligation, constructs a naturalistic and expressly anti-rule and anti-political ethics of care.

The central role of the motherchild relation, and her observations about gender differences in approaches to moral problems prompt Noddings to call her ethic of care a 'feminine ethic'. Although she does not 'imply a claim for all women or ... exclude men' from her ethics of care, Noddings does argue that 'there is reason to believe that women are somewhat better equipped for caring than men are'.

Thus the ethics of care are tied, in this formulation, to femininity and women's experience of the private sphere. Noddings's account is naturalistic because she links the development of a 'moral imperative' to care to what she sees as an innate 'impulse to act on behalf of the present other'. This innate impulse is fostered into the capacity for moral awareness and judgement by a cycle of caring relationships that starts with the natural care a mother gives a child. When we are confronted with someone in need, she argues, the 'memory of our own best moments of caring and being cared for sweeps over us as a feeling—as an "I must"—in response to the plight of the other and our conflicting desire to serve our own interests'. However, she continues:

> we are not compelled by this impulse. We have a choice; we may accept what we feel, or we may reject it. If we have a strong desire to be moral, we will not reject it, and this strong desire to be moral is derived, reflectively, from the more fundamental and natural desire to be and to remain related.

When we are faced with moral decisions about how to act as 'one-caring', Noddings argues that reference to moral principles can be a positive barrier to care; hence our designation 'anti-rule'. Discussing moral conduct by exploring language and reasoning, she contends, takes us

> away from an assessment of the concrete events in which we must choose whether and how to behave morally. Indeed we are often led far beyond what we feel and intuitively judge to be right in a search for some simple and absolute guide to moral goodness.

We characterise Noddings's approach as anti-political because of the way she constructs the scope and limits of our obligation to care as 'limited and delimited by relation':

> We are never free, in the human domain, to abandon our preparedness to care; but, practically, if we are meeting those in our inner circles adequately as ones-caring and receiving those linked to our inner circles by formal chains of relation, we shall limit the calls upon our obligation quite naturally.

Constructing the scope of moral action in this way emphasises the local and contingent, placing a strong imperative on moral agents to engage practically with our fellow human beings in very day-to-day ways. This leads Noddings to express active hostility to institutions, and to claim that a child whose mother teaches him moral reasoning well will go out into the world 'skeptical, vulnerable, courageous, disobedient, and tenderly receptive'.

Other feminist theorists of the ethic of care take issue with approaches like Noddings's, which emphasise the role of natural care and the mother-child relationship, suspect reasoning and rules in moral inquiry, and narrowly circumscribe the limits on the obligation to care to personal relationships. Instead, more recent contributions by Selma Sevenhuijsen and Joan Tronto to the discourse of the ethics of care have emphasised the need to move beyond oppositional thinking (masculine versus feminine, care versus justice, relationship versus rules) in debates about feminist ethics, to 'denaturalise' the ethics of care, and to integrate thinking about the ethics of care with political theory and activity on a much broader stage than interpersonal relationships.

Again, the metaphor of a web is useful to capture the key arguments and their relationships. Much that distinguishes the contributions of these theorists ramifies from their position that care is necessarily a political as well as a moral concept, such that power and difference are central. From this perspective, answers to the questions of 'who cares?' and 'whose needs are met?' go well beyond identifying the dyad of the 'one-caring' and the 'present other in need'. Rather, at the 'macro' level of society as whole, and at the 'micro' level of interpersonal relationships, the 'politicised' approach to the ethics of care explores how the ethics of care both can illuminate problems of power and difference in existing social arrangements, and can help overcome some of the characteristic problems and dilemmas of care that unequal power engenders.

At the macro level, answers to these questions explore how class, gender, ability and race interact to distribute both the getting and giving of care. Typically, the powerful 'are more often in a position to receive or demand care than to provide it', while those with less power often find themselves 'in situations in which they provide care without much power over the conditions and the means, and often in positions of invisibility and voicelessness'.

This recognition also allows these theorists to shed light on the 'dark side' of care at the micro level. Tronto highlights two 'dangers of care': paternalism/maternalism and parochialism. She describes the first as follows:

> Often care-givers have more competence and expertise in meeting the needs of those receiving care. The result is that care-givers may well come to see themselves as more capable of assessing the needs of carereceivers than are the care-receivers themselves.
>
> ...Especially when the caregivers' sense of importance, duty, career, etc., are tied to their caring role, we can well imagine the development of relationships of profound inequality.

Parochialism results from care when we see the caring relationships in which we are engaged, and which we know best as the most important. Here Tronto highlights the particular hazard of the use of the mother child relationship as the founding metaphor of the ethics of care. She writes 'A Mother who did not think that her child's needs were more important than another child's would seem incompetent', yet if we construct a political ideal on this basis, care 'could quickly become a way to argue that everyone should cultivate one's own garden, and let others take care of themselves, too'.

However, Tronto and Sevenhuijsen argue that a political approach to the ethics of care also offers remedies for these problems of care. For example, the relational ontology of the ethics of care exposes the inequality and oppression in the existing social division of caring by highlighting that all humans are dependent on others; yet the distribution of the costs and benefits of care does not adequately reflect need and capacity to give. In a similar vein, the emphasis on what Walker, cited above, called 'shared processes of discovery, expression, interpretation, and adjustment between persons' reflects the democratic impulse of the ethics of care. As Tronto puts it, care

> can serve as a political concept to prescribe an ideal for more democratic, more pluralistic politics...in which power is more evenly distributed. ... care can [also] serve as a strategic concept to involve directly the relatively disenfranchised in the political world.

Finally, in addition to linking caring to critiques of current social structures, and to new ways of thinking about negotiating power, privilege, and difference, politicised constructions of the ethics of care do not reject rights and justice as categories of moral and political discourse. Rather, theorists like Tronto and Sevenhuijsen both seek to bring to bear the insights and methods of the ethics of care to reframe justice ethics, and see that care requires rights to be fully realised.

Social Work and Ethics of Care

Engagement between social work and the ethics of care involves both opportunities and risks for both social workers and service users. Many social workers would recognise their working relationships with service users either in reality or in aspiration in the descriptions of the nature of moral response and action offered in the discourses of the ethics of care. The insights of the ethics of care support and articulate social workers' self-understanding as moral agents in caring relationships with service users. As a feminist discourse, the ethics of care provides the conceptual space and a vocabulary for recognising and valuing care absent from rational-technical approaches to knowledge and practice, whether professional, bureaucratic, or managerialist.

This has implications for the recognition of the value and efficacy of social work both in service management and wider social contexts, including current attempts to 'modernise'. As an account of decision-making in interpersonal interactions, the ethics of care also provides a gender-sensitive, moral ground to concepts of reflective practice to develop further existing alternatives to rationaltechnical models. Thus, the ethics of care offers social work theory and practice what might be called an 'epistemological' opportunity. In describing interactions as 'shared processes of discovery, expression, interpretation, and adjustment between persons', the ethics of care also supports social work's commitment to dialogic relations between social workers and service users. In effect, the ethics of care enhances social workers' capacity to achieve the goals of those with whom they work and the recognition of the value of social work as both a service discipline and a set of practices. It offers a sophisticated framework for including aspects of social work practice and experience that have recently been difficult to encompass, and so to teach, learn, justify, and develop.

However, despite the 'opportunities' described above, it is probably not a coincidence that the notion of care has received little recent attention in social work. The critical social work literature comes close to identifying care with oppression. At a minimum it is seen as patronising, paternalist, and marginalising. Historically care has been associated with 'the welfare', being 'looked after', or 'protected' so that service users are seen as little more than dependent recipients of care. Care is also associated with charity for which those on the receiving end should be grateful.

More recently, service user activism and social work discourses have emphasised the importance of user involvement, partnership, participation, rights, and, perhaps most significantly, empowerment. The contemporary use of the term 'service user' as opposed to 'client' symbolises this change in emphasis. From this perspective, care is very much associated with a past that social work is trying to 'modernise'. To suggest that social work should look afresh at ideas about care, even in the context of debates about the ethics of care, could be seen as at best naïve and at worst dangerous. Not only might it have the unintended consequence of reinforcing the existing prejudices and problems arising from the cultural and political devaluation of the feminine in a context where caring work is female dominated, but it may deflect attention from what service user movements say they want.

Focussing on the disability movement, Fiona Williams has recently explored some challenging critiques of the ethics of care that focus on the risks of conceptualising service interactions as care from a service user perspective.

First, she notes that rejecting care, Wood argues for empowerment particularly where it emphasises choice and control, while Finkelstein argues that care is now so laden it should be replaced by support.

Secondly, Williams points out that while the ethics of care emphasises interdependence and the relational, 'disabled people have argued for the strategic centrality of independence, tying it to the practical demand for independent living in which autonomy and control over one's life are key'. So, for example, rather than dependence on a professional or a case-manager for services, direct payments and personal assistance schemes provide service users with the power to 'purchase' their own services.

Thirdly, she considers Silvers's argument that to propose that the mutuality and closeness of family life become the paradigm in social life fails to grasp how the power inherent in extra-familial care relationships is not attenuated by the tenderness of intimacy. Williams sees Silvers's conclusion to be that the ethics of care deflects from the paradigm of equality, and it is equality, not care, 'that can both contain the demands for civil rights for disabled people, as well as connect to the struggles of other marginalised groups'.

These critics are responding to what Tronto identifies as the 'dark side' of care. However, we agree with Williams that service user critiques of the ethics of care share more common ground with the views they seem to oppose than may first appear, particularly when the diversity of positions within the ethics of care debate is taken into account. Moreover, Williams identifies a problem with some disability movement theory, which, she argues, overestimates the extent to which relationships are fixedly structured around domination (by carers) and subordination (of the cared for).

As proponents of the ethics of care suggest, 'we can in practice be carers or cared-for in different situations and do not always occupy one single position in this binary'. Further, both the ethics of care approach, as elaborated by Tronto and Sevenhuijsen, and the empowerment approach, as elaborated by writers like Beresford, operate within an equality paradigm. In their 'politicised' version, both Tronto and Sevenhuijsen stress the importance of the principles of equality and justice in the development and application of the ethics of care. Care is not simply a micro-moral issue but is necessarily political and is intimately related to wider structural issues concerned with class, gender, ability, and race.

Williams also points out that despite different emphases in their understandings of autonomy/ independence, writers from within the disability movement and proponents of the politicised ethics of care both make the important distinction between the inadequate conceptualisation of autonomy as self-sufficiency, and autonomy/independence as the capacity to have choice and control over one's life. Williams herself argues that the concept of interdependence, which is so central to the ethics of care, needs to recognise that recent collective struggles around care place a premium on independence. She continues:

> it is possible to argue that, in the longer term, disabled peoples' interests would be better served by a society that valued interdependence and acknowledged the

> vulnerability of all, the more immediate strategy for disabled people is for rights to secure the conditions for independence. The task then becomes less one of arguing against autonomy as a liberal concept than one of redefining the concept of autonomy to fit with a notion of interdependence'.

Finally, Williams explores how the issue of professional versus non-professional paid care for disabled people exposes another risk and opportunity of the ethics of care. Too much emphasis on the quality of the relationship between the carer and the person cared for rather than the carer's training and expertise, and the assumption that professional carers are 'inculcated with ... paternalism ... overlaps dangerously with arguments that have kept women workers low paid for generations—that they bring with them skills which are 'natural' and need not be valued'.

Rather than seek the putatively unsullied care of untrained carers, Williams argues that the skills of care should be claimed as skills, 'and that the issue is how to develop training so that the knowledge and experience of disabled people and other service users influence work practices'. From this perspective, the risks of the personalised version of the ethics of care can be avoided by a more politicised approach.

Work in the UK by the National Institute for Social Work and Peter Beresford and his colleagues in this context is very instructive. As part of the debate on the future of social work in England, social work practitioners, people whose primary responsibility was to work with and be in close contact with service users themselves, came together to identify what was seen as the key characteristics of best social work practice. There was considerable overlap and consistency in terms of: a holistic approach to social and personal problem solving; a relationship based on respect; attention to the experience of individuals, groups, and communities and to their expertise, culture, and religion; recognition that the process and the relationship is part of what determines a good outcome for service users; access to independent information on which to think through options and reach decisions; service users retaining as much control as possible over their lives and the choices they make. From this, Peter Beresford then argues that 'practice that is emancipatory and liberating needs a value base that is shared between practitioners and people using services. A jointly developed human rights and citizenship framework offers this possibility'.

While debate about the ethics of care has been significantly informed by fundamental criticisms of the individualised liberal ethics of rights, it is our view that, in drawing on the politicised variant of the ethics of care, it is not helpful to see approaches based on rights/empowerment in such stark antithesis to those based on care. As Orme has recently argued, drawing on Gilligan, Jagger and Hekman, justice and care are logically compatible and indispensable to each other, and that a dialogical approach challenges binaries not only of the carer/cared for, the public/private, but that between care and justice and rights.

It is in this spirit that we feel the ethics of care provide a key critical framework for both analysing and moving beyond the current dominance of the managerialist approaches to social work. In doing so not only are we more able to see the central relevance of grappling with care theoretically and practically, but the attempts to 'modernise' will themselves have a greater chance to deliver on a range of key objectives and principles which are currently in danger of being lost. The aim to overcome the divide between rationality and the emotions in much moral, political, and epistemological thought can prove productive in the current climate. It proposes a different kind of moral decision-making, in which both a different 'cognitive attitude' and a different 'form of action' underpin different kinds of moral decisionmaking where experience, relationships, and contexts become key.

Organisation of Social Work

The transformation of collective life has influenced the tasks of social work, and made it much more difficult to practice effectively. The textbooks on values, aims and methods still talk about 'anti-oppressive approaches', about 'integration', 'cohesion' and 'inclusion'. But it is not at all clear how social work techniques and strategies can counteract the long-term effects on disadvantaged districts of the changes, or can best address the tasks of integrating and including those whose nomadism has caused fragmentation, confusion, isolation or conflict. Neither the exclusion of whole communities from new forms of cosmopolitan economic membership, occupied by skilled and resourceful households, voting with their feet to enter well-appointed 'communities of choice', nor the failure of others who move in search of these forms of membership, but do not establish adequate supportive bonds, are easily addressed by existing methods.

The organisation of social work is coming both to reflect this transformation, and to reinforce its consequences. Here again, its situation is much the same as that of other human service professions, but the consequences for social work are more profound. The logic which informs the 'modernisation' of these services, especially in the US and UK, but increasingly also in Continental Europe, is that citizens should be able to make 'informed choices' about their subscriptions to the systems that supply these goods. This implies that they should have rights and opportunities to switch between systems, according to the return they receive on their contributions. This logic is highly compatible with the strategies, based on commercial-style exit options rather than participation and democratic voice.

The economic theory which informs this model – public choice theory of 'fiscal federalism' – involves the transformation of public and publicly-funded services, on two dimensions. On the one hand, new technologies of various kinds allow goods which were previously difficult to divide up and allocate to individuals to be provided instead to members of exclusive 'clubs'. The latter is the technical term for those who, by subscribing to membership schemes or networks are able to obtain certain services at a special price, and from which non-subscribers are excluded. Various kinds of electronic and other technology make it far easier nowadays to set up such 'clubs', and hence make commercial or quasi-commercial organisations (public-private initiatives) economically viable, where previously only inclusive state provision was feasible. Hence 'modernisation' often entails allowing commercial companies to finance or manage previously public services, or to provide them under contract to the government. 'Clubs' of this kind are often transnational, so patients from one country are treated in hospitals in another.

The second aspect is that local authorities compete with each other to attract taxpaying residents, by providing a bundle of collective amenities and services that are attractive to households in various income brackets. This implies that mobile and well-informed households move between such jurisdictions, maximising their gains in terms of welfare returns on local taxes and accommodation costs. In the UK, the government has insisted on the publication of increasingly sophisticated league tables of 'value for money' and service outcomes, by education authorities, schools, hospitals and health care trusts. This encourages 'voting with the feet' by resourceful citizens, but it also enables those with adequate incomes and few needs to segregate themselves from those with low incomes and many needs, thus consolidating disadvantages and concentrating deprivation. Where – by expensive state intervention – higher standards are achieved in schools or hospitals serving poor areas, this is quickly changed, since better-off people move in, and queuing for places shifts the worse-off to the back of the line.

Taken together, these two aspects represent a formidable challenge to social work practice. The policies emerging in all First World states tend to consolidate the impact of global economic forces, by reforming and restructuring local and national government agencies, and the funding of non-government bodies, in line with fiscal federalist principles, and requiring local jurisdictions to compete with each other for the sake of 'efficiency' and 'choice'. But there is yet another aspect of this agenda, whose impact is only beginning to be felt, and which has even more radical implications.

Under the World Trade Organisation's General Agreement on Trade in Services (GATS), currently in the process of being negotiated and implemented, the public sectors of all states will gradually be opened up for competition between state agencies, hybrid partnerships and private firms, including firms from outside the country. What has already happened in the European Union for water, gas and electricity supplies, with provision in the UK by French firms, will extend to health, education and personal social services. Large specialist companies will seek to win contracts to take over these functions, either in partnership with existing providers, or in their own right.

The World Trade Organisation, under attack from anti-globalisation and anti-capitalist protests, and stung by criticism from human rights organisations and non-government bodies, has insisted that there will be many safeguards in this process. Governments will be able to control the pace and sequencing of opening their public sectors to this competition and privatisation, and will be permitted to regulate standards. However, the fact remains that the destination envisaged by GATS is a global market in health, education and welfare services, albeit a regulated, and partly publicly funded one. Furthermore, when the process starts, countries will be faced with hard choices over whether to enter the field as 'predators' (backing international companies based in their territory to take over services in other states) or as 'prey'. The USA and UK have already decided on the former option. In the UK, for instance, it is clear that 'modernisation' programmes, based on ideas of fiscal federalism, favour the entry of private firms into the provision of public services in this sector, for finance, management and delivery.

For social work and its service users, this has fairly radical implications. Already the field of social care and especially its residential sector, has seen the entry of international companies, providing a range of facilities. Such firms bring a new commercial ethos to the task, often employing young and inexperienced staff, on part-time contracts, but locating their management structures in centralised offices far from these facilities. Furthermore, commercialisation has made the whole supply of services volatile, as it responds to price factors as well as to demand.

Mirroring the globalisation of social care services, the recruitment crisis in public services has been addressed by recruitment of professional staff from all over the English-speaking world, and beyond. As with teachers nurses and doctors, social workers from other countries are sought to meet specific shortages, especially in large cities, where housing costs are high, and many indigenous professionals cannot afford to accommodate their families. Many highly sensitive social work services are staffed by such recruits who, whatever their professional skills, are necessarily unfamiliar with law, regulations and public service cultures.

The transformation of the organisation of social work raises questions about the relationship of practice to the collective life of society. In the era of welfare states, public service staff gained a certain prestige and respect from the fact that their activities reflected the commitment of the society to its members, and the personal attention that they could receive for their special needs, from a caring state. Although most staff did not work for the government, some of the same ethos of representing the collective commitment of the community to the welfare of all rubbed off on them. Commercial care is different; it involves buying into a form of membership which supplies a product to a customer, under conditions where individual welfare depends on relationship with others, but where the costs associated with sharing are minimised. It is difficult to see how the ethos of social citizenship and the common good, which has underpinned most social work values and practices in the postwar era, can survive such a transformation.

7

Evidence-based Social Work

Evidence-based practice (EBP) originated within the medical school of McMaster University, Toronto, in the early 1990s. By definition, evidence-based medicine (EBM) involves the conscientious, explicit, and judicious application of best research evidence to a range of domains: clinical examinations, diagnostic tests, prognostic markers, and the safety and efficacy of interventions whose purposes may be therapeutic, rehabilitative, or preventative, with therapeutic interventions understandably getting most of the attention.

Besides best research evidence, EBM has two other elements: clinical expertise and patient values. Currently, EBM focuses primarily on locating and evaluating research evidence. In efforts to foster the application of best evidence to medical practice, medical groups have developed journals and online resources that provide practice guidelines, reviews of research, and bibliographies.

EBM is laid out in a neat and orderlyway, with a painstakingly described set of five steps that compose its practice, a list of questions to answer when following each of these steps, flow charts, a classification of evidence in terms of its relevance and value, and careful descriptions of blind, randomised clinical trials (RCTs) as the gold standard for deciding the efficacy of interventions. RCTs are called experimental designs in the social sciences.

EBM relies heavily on quantitative indicators, such as confidence intervals, effect size, experimental event rate, control over event rate, and number needed to be treated to prevent one event. Guyatt et al. for theEBMWG recommended the quantification of both evidence and values, stating this is "the most rigorous approach to making recommendations". Evidence about diagnosis, prognosis, or harm can arise from other forms of research besides RCTs, including case studies and qualitative research.

Evidence about the efficacy of interventions whose face validity is self-evident and whose withholding poses ethical issues do not require RCTs. Face validity means expert practitioners conclude that the intervention works and meets ethical standards. EBM requires giving up procedures and tests when evidence suggests that new approaches are safer, more efficacious, and accurate. For example, the cause of stomach ulcers was once thought to be stress or spicy foods, whereas today there is strong evidence that bacteria are the causative agents.

As a result, treatment for stomach ulcers has changed. Research-based evidence informs but does not replace clinical expertise, which is the basis of judgments as to how research findings are used with individual clients. Clinical expertise is the knowledge physicians have accumulated through their medical practice in identification of patient's state of health, in diagnosis, and in the assessment of individual risk factors and potential benefits of possible interventions.

In addition to clinical expertise, the application of research evidence to individuals requires knowledge of patients' values. Patients' values include the expectations, concerns, and preferences that patients bring with them. In using the term patient values, EBM has joined itself to person-centered medicine (PCM), where the term patient values is a core concept. PCM is based on humanistic perspectives related to the work of Balint, Rogers, and nursing theorists Neuman and Young, among others. A key aspect of PCM is the understanding and accommodation of patient values in clinical practice and the need for practitioners to be aware of their own values.

Challenges of EBM

Contemporary EBM is a rational-technical model that also recognises humanistic issues related to practice. Though clinical expertise and patient values are elements, the handbook on the practice of EBM and many other writings specific to EBM focus attention on locating, evaluating, and applying research to clinical problems, with special emphasis on therapeutic interventions.

EBM has many limitations. Limitations include not only underconceptualisations of patients'values and of physicians' clinical expertise, but also of how the personal perspectives of physicians affect clinical practice. The challenges that physicians confront in locating and using research evidence also limit the effectivenes of efforts to make medicine more evidence-based, meaning based on research. Finally, the effectiveness of EBM is difficult to document, though the importance of applying research evidence to practice is widely acknowledged as selfevident.

At present, the Evidence-Based MedicineWorking Group (EBMWG)has expended little effort toward delineating the implications of what it means to incorporate patients' values. For example, Sackett et al. interrupted their step-by-step description of EBM by briefly discussing the importance of patients' experiences of medical treatment. They pointed to the capacities of qualitative research to shed light on "patients' feelings, ideas and wider experience rather than measuring objective outcomes". Nurse-researchers, they said, have taken the lead in bringing qualitative understandings into the health sciences.

Many groups and individuals, beyond those who are members of the EBMWG, are moving toward enlarging understandings of patients' values. By using the term patient values, the EBMWG has joined EBM to PCM, which involves careful exploration of patients' experiences with illness. This includes impact on daily personal and family functioning and on families' and patients' expectations about what ought to be done medically. The goal is to find common ground with patients and respond to patients'unique concerns.

Being patient-centered is a core value for many physicians, and it contrasts with medicine that is illness centered or doctor-centered. The pragmatic and humanistic bases of patient-centered care is summed up in Hart's statement that health is the product of health care, and patients are one of the producers, not simply customers. Some physicians are advocating more sensitivity to patients' religious and cultural values, expectations, and preferences.

Epstein responded to gaps in the conceptualisation ofEBM by proposing the concept of mindfulness as a bridge between PCM and EBM. Mindfulness directs attention to both practitioners' and patients' values and beliefs. It posits that physicians must be aware of their own cultural and religious values if they are to be responsive to patients. Thus, Epstein focused primarily on the person of the physician and on mindful practice. Mindful practitioners seek self-knowledge because, without it, physicians cannot practice "core values in medicine, such as empathy, compassion, and altruism".

Mindful practice also draws on many sources of information. Its goals are "compassionate informed action in the world," the use of a "wide array of data," "correct decisions," understanding the patient, and the relief of suffering. Besides the person of the physician, mindful practice encompasses patients as persons with whom physicians form relationships. Values in mindful practice include both "ethical self-awareness" that shape medical encounters and "technical self-awareness," which leads to "self-correction" during the course of doing medicine. Mindful practitioners also recognise the uncertainty and ambiguity inherent in clinical practice and research evidence. Problem-solving and the capacity to challenge one's own assumptions and prejudices characterise mindful practice.

Epstein noted that clinical expertise is often based on tacit knowledge, where clinical actions and decision making stems from unarticulated premises and understandings. Mindful practice will help make the implicit more explicit, and, as is widely recognised, tacit knowledge is characteristic of practice. Ideas related to tacit knowledge in professions is quite different from a rational, quantified model represented by EBM. Practice can be messy, subjective, and ambiguous. Still, relevant research evidence is of obvious importance, as is widely acknowledged among commentators on EBM.

Epstein has a lot of company in his quest to highlight the importance of the person of the physician. Sweeney, MacAuley, and Gray coined the term "personal significance," referring to the meanings doctors and patients bring to bear in making decisions about courses of actions. In their analysis, doctors' logical thinking, intuition, personal background, and personal experience influence clinical decision making. As doctors gain in experience, the processes that organise their practice become more a matter of "script recognition" and "historical pattern analysis" rather than primarily rational and analytic.

Nature of Evidence and Practice

Notable is Epstein's perspectives on the nature of evidence. He stated that the "knowledge, skills, values, and experience" that "seasoned practitioners" bring to bear on clinical decision making is "a different kind of evidence". In this framework, clinical judgment becomes an interpretive process that is both science and art, the art related to processes of bringing together these many kinds of evidence to make decisions. Others, too, acknowledge medical practice as an art, as when Guyatt et al. stated that clinical decisions "involve an implicit consideration of the relevant evidence, an intuitive integration of the evidence, and a weighing of the likely benefits and harms". Godlee cited Clasziou's case study as an example of the art of using research evidence in particular cases, in this instance, to solve the mystery of a nonsmoking woman's 20-year cough.

Epstein's views of what constitutes evidence differ markedly from definitions in EBM, which in most cases implies that the term applies only to research evidence. The EBMWG and other proponents have no formal definition of evidence. When the term is defined in medicine, its scope varies from narrow to broad. Miettinen defined evidence as "the published report of a single piece of original research". Evidence in this sense is that which is produced by a scientific study. On the other hand, Goodman and Royall offered a broader definition: "evidence is the basis on which we derive inferences". This view is close to dictionary definitions: "1. The data on which a judgment can be based or proof established. 2. That which serves to indicate".

Some have found that medical practice can accommodate both the systematic, mathematical, and precise understandings of what EBM considers scientific evidence, as well as the more interpretive, ambiguous, personalised evidence that arises in patient-physician interactions. For example, Upshur noted, "evidence in health is neither exclusively abstract, mathematical, and general nor narrative and particular, but is a mediation and interaction of both types of knowledge". Smith integrated patient-centered interviewing with evidencebased approaches. Depending on the medical situation, one type of knowledge may carry more weight than another. In general, however, some medical practitioners believe both types of knowledge can work together to provide competent medical care, a view that Upshur, Smith, and Epstein represent.

For Epstein, mindful critical reflection can help identify and manage personal bias. Such a stance includes developing capacities for challenging assumptions and preferred ways of viewing the self, others, and the world. Other physicians, such as Green, also recognise a variety of types of bias, such as "optimistic bias," or the belief that our interventions are more effective than actuality—also known as seeing what is not there—and "advocacy bias," which is the desire of researchers to see positive results. Guyatt et al., as part of the EBMWG, on the other hand, stated that the systematic following of the steps of EBM can protect against bias. They appear to overlook the possibility that personal perspectives shape interpretations of even the most rigorous research and the most painstakingly followed procedures, as Green suggested.

Limitations of Research Evidence

The EBMWG and the wider practice and academic communities recognise the limitations of research evidence, while, at the same time, they stress the obvious value of using evidence when it is available. Research evidence can be inconclusive, contradictory, controversial, nonexistent, and difficult to apply to individual cases. Controversies about the efficacy of treatment are common. An example is the questioning of the evidence supporting mammography. The unsettled nature of research evidence, as Sackett et al. noted, is not specific to EBM but is universal to applied and basic science.

When research evidence is unavailable or inconclusive, physicians are operating in a grey zone that requires the use of "clinical experience and reasoning", though they did not specify what these principles might be. Such situations generate "a supremely pragmatic agenda for applied health research", which puts a positive perspective on a lack of research evidence, a serious issue.

Some physicians are concerned about the emphasis in EBM on medical outcomes for individuals, without also taking into account social and economic conditions such as poverty and its consequences. These conditions lead to more illness and premature death among the poor than among the better off. Medical research that takes social conditions into account may provide the kinds of evidence that will improve health care among the poor.

Who funds medical research also generates wide discussion. For example, Dieppe, Chard, Tallon, and Egger noted that pharmaceutical companies have undue influence not only on what medical conditions and interventions are researched but also on how likely the research is to be published. Dieppe et al. suggested that doctors consult with patients to decide which interventions are to be researched and then look for means of funding such research.

Searching for best evidence can be time-consuming, even when physicians have training in locating, evaluating, and applying research evidence. Proponents recognise this challenge and have developed many online resources, as noted earlier, including the Cochrane Database of Systematic Reviews, Medline, and Best Evidence. Yet doctors sometimes do not use easily accessed evidence.

Many factors appear to affect take-up of new therapies, including both patients' and physicians' perceptions that some medications are harmful, even when research evidence shows they are not, physicians' lack of direct exposure to the efficacy of new treatments, and lack of promotion from pharmaceutical companies because the treatments generate little revenue.

Practice Guidelines

In addition, online and journal resources have generated concerns in terms of quality, possible bias, and implications for workload. Eisenberg, a general practitioner, found that new practice guidelines for the prevention of coronary disease lowered the threshold for who is considered at risk and, thus, increased many times over the number of office visits that the new guidelines required, while having little, if any, identifiable impact on patients' health. Drummond said these guidelines do not take into account considerations related to race and ethnicity. Still, othersworry about the quality of the information in some of the databases. The EBMWG both acknowledges and responds to concerns. For example, the proponents of EBM recognised the difficulty of applying research evidence to individual patient situations. The editors of the British Medical Journal commissioned case studies to show how the steps of EBM can be applied to clinical practice.

EBM may raise the cost of care because of its emphasis on efficacy. The most efficacious treatments may be expensive. When costs of patients'care comes from government sources or insurance companies, where funds are finite, this raises ethical issues. If a great deal of money is expended for a relatively small number of patients, questions arise as to how to provide for the large number of other patients, whose care also is financed from limited resources. Conversely, if patients do not receive care because of the expense, this is an ethical issue as well.

Ironically, there may be no way of applying the gold standard of randomised clinical trials to evaluate the effectiveness of EBM. Such an experiment would involve random assignment into treatment and control groups. The treatment group would receive interventions based on research evidence, and the control group would not. Instead, the control group would receive interventions based on clinical expertise. Such a study would be unethical. It would also have severe issues with construct validity of both the treatment and control variables. Regarding treatment variables, it would be impossible to isolate the effects of research-based evidence from other possible causes, such as clinical expertise and patients'values and expectations.

For the control variables, clinical expertise is an amalgam of what practitioners have learned from their clinical experience, what they already know from research and theories, and their own personal values and perspectives. These confounding influences could not be disentangled. The effectiveness issue may have to be decided on the basis of logic. Few would argue that practitioners should not use research evidence when it is available. There are indicators that the teaching ofEBMis having positive influences, though evaluations, arguably, are in early stages. For example, evidence-based teaching methods in postgraduate medical education improves performance more than traditional didactic methods. Yew, on the other hand, found in a small 3-year follow-up study that most graduates of a residency program did not use the skills of EBM that the program emphasized. The pressures of time, money, and family responsibilities were issues, as well as finding internet resources unhelpful. Colleagues were the usual sources of information because this was quick and easy.

In addition, the Centre for Evidence-Based Child Health, which has an extensive training program for professionals already in practice, has yet to evaluate the effectiveness of their programs beyond a postprogram evaluation. Finally, a study in a general hospital with university affiliations found that most clinical interventions are based on best research evidence, whereas others wonder whether EBM is of value to academics, but practicing clinicians do not widely accept it because of its emphasis on the written word and, consequently, the time it takes to "forage through a jungle of information".

Proponents have devoted considerable expertise and energy to EBM. They advocate for the application of research evidence to practice, while upholding the centrality of clinical expertise and patient values. They have developed several types of resources that make evidence available to clinical practitioners, and they respond to criticism in constructive ways. Who funds research and what interest such funders have in the results are serious ethical issues that merit much reflection and discussion in social work.

Some physicians, who often are not strongly associated with the development of EBM, are helping to delineate underdeveloped elements of EBM, such as the implications of and meanings assigned to clinical expertise, patient values, and the perspectives that physicians bring to their practice.

EBM is a work in progress, with proponents open to suggestions for improving its usefulness and efficacy. Its practice is not fixed but is evolving as physicians and other health care professionals gain experience in following its procedures. There are many questions, including issues related to quality of research evidence, on howto foster the use of evidence when it is available, and on how to allocate limited resources. Nowhere within medicine are there calls not to use research in practice. How to use research evidence and what types of research that are available are at issue.

Evidence-Based Nursing

The experiences of nurses with EBP are similar to those of doctors, in terms of both optimism and cautions. Nursing is a profession of caring and emphasizes relationships and humanistic values. In general, evidence-based nursing follows the procedures of EBM). Similar to doctors, nurses have centers for EBP throughout the world.

The application of research findings to nursing practice is of unquestioned importance. Some have pointed out that besides the obvious ethical obligation to use the best available information, nursing as a profession will gain both in influence and credibility if its practices are shown to be grounded in research. Nurses, however, appear to be more forthright about issues related to RCTs, more openly critical of some of the assumptions of EBM that many call positivistic, and more willing to insist that management provide both time and resources for nurses to pursue best evidence.

Many nurses are thinking about the implications of nursing's holistic philosophy for EBP. This holistic philosophy provided the context for other nurses to state that much of EBP is based on positivistic assumptions that is concerned with "what can be measured, touched, and enumerated". Hamer worried about the potential for these assumptions to overlook experiences, feelings, and attitudes. She concluded that discussions and debates about EBP need to acknowledge that the dominance of any one perspective could lead to the exclusion of other perspectives that are actually integral to patient care.

In light of these holistic perspectives, in addition, Rafael questioned whether the effectiveness of evidence-based nursing can ever be measured because nursing effectiveness cannot be isolated from "the therapeutic and caring relationship that is foundational to nursing practice". Santy pointed out that nurses require training in howto evaluate the usefulness and applicability of research evidence to individual patients.

Some nurses have pointed out that EBP is a form of research utilization, a concern in nursing for more than 30 years. As such, the barriers to EBP are enduring. Nursing management has major roles to play in lowering these barriers. These solutions to barriers include developing research that is accessible and meaningful to nurse practitioners, providing training for nurses in the interpretation and application of research, and providing nurses with the time and resources to search out best research evidence.

Evidence-Based Social Work Practices

Evidence-based social work is far more established in the United Kingdom than in the United States. Not only are there extended discussions of the implications and meanings of EBP, but the government has funded a Centre on Evidence-Based Social Services that has sponsored several studies with promise of relevance to practice. These studies include the evaluation of the effectiveness of foster parent training for reducing disruptions, a review of French, German, and Italian social work literature, and an evaluation of a family conferencing project.

Many of the issues that interest English social workers are similar to those in medicine and nursing. For example, there is recognition of the idea that choices of research methods depend on what researchers want to know and that experimental designs (or RCTs), when feasible and well conducted, do provide the most valid tests of the effectiveness of interventions. Other forms of research are needed for other areas of social work practice, such as the use of qualitative research for understanding clients' situations. Sheldon and Macdonald label debates on the merits of qualitative and quantitative research as false. As in medicine and nursing, English socialworkers, such as Sheppard et al. are suggesting ways to create practice that acknowledges the importance of research evidence, even when such evidence has large gaps and is patchy.

English social workers appear to have overlooked the idea that EBP is composed of more than the application of research evidence to practice. As both the nurses and doctors have pointed out, the elements of EBP include clinical expertise, clients' perspectives, and the personal perspectives that practitioners bring to situations, as discussed earlier. Despite this, the thinking of English social workers contributes to a social-work specific form of EBP.

Certainly, no responsible social worker would state that we should not use relevant research in our practice. When relevant research is available, professional and personal ethics require that we use it. For some conditions, there is clear and convincing evidence that particular interventions are effective. These interventions tend to be those with a biological substrate, such as mental disorders, and are amenable to cognitive-behavioral therapy in combination with medication.

Yet in work with clients, social workers need to know far more than what is available in research reports. Therefore, in addition to relevant research, we have to depend on values as represented in the National Association of Social Workers Code of Ethics, theories, assumptions, nonexperimental research, professional experience, and personal experience, all of which is tailored to individual client systems. Competent practitioners, therefore, draw on a wide array of sources. They fit what they know to client situations, and they change their assumptions and approaches in response to clients'responses to their efforts.

Social work has contended with the challenges of research diffusion and utilization for many years. Diffusion and utilization connect to basic orientations to practice. Is social work best viewed as a positivistic endeavor? Are clients responsive to prescriptive practice and expert systems? Fewsocialworkers advocate the mindless application of prescriptions to individual clients. Few social workers state that we should not be reflective on our practice and on how our personal views affect howwe do our practice. Respect for client preferences,wants, and cultures appears to be close universal. No social worker states that we should not use research when it is available. No one can put up a respectable argument that we should fly by the seat of our pants and use untested assumptions on clients. We do not have research for all of the issues that any one client wants to deal with or is forced to deal with in nonvoluntary situations. Socialworkers drawon multiple sources.

Because social workers bring the first three elements into practice situations before they ever meet a newclient, they must be on guard not to impose these ideas on clients but be ready, willing, and even eager for clients to falsify their ideas and assumptions. Falsification involves the development of hypotheses about situations and refutation and reformulation of these hypotheses by what occurs in the situations. It makes sense for social workers to have hypotheses about prospective clients based on what they have learned from other practitioners, what they know from research and theory, what they have read in case records, and what they know in general about clients in similar situations. In addition, acknowledgement of how personal values and viewpoints influence practice is a hallmark of ethical practice. To connect with clients, however, social workers hold these hypotheses lightly, seeking to examine their fit and then modify them or even discard them when working with clients. Discarding leads to the formulation of new hypotheses, which then are tested in interaction with clients.

Effective practitioners base their work on conceptual frameworks drawn from the best available research and theory and from practice experience-their own and what they can learn from colleagues. In addition, they reflect on their personal ideologies, values, and assumptions and howthey influence what we see and expect to see, howwe think, and how we respond to others. Often, our values, beliefs, and assumptions derive not only from our interpretations of our interpersonal relationships but also from what we absorb from popular culture, such as television, movies, and print media, and from poetry, drama, novels, art, and music. Our cultural heritage also affects our senseof self and how we view the world, though we may not be aware of these influences.

The experiences of other practice professions have a great deal to offer social work practice. Like medicine, nursing, social work practice will benefit from increased research activity, more widespread availability of reviews of research, online resources, and many more training opportunities. Like nursing administrators, social work administrators have the responsibility to allow social worker practitioners to have the time to become familiar with research relevant to their practice. Funders have a great influence on whether this is possible. Unfortunately, with the massive cutbacks in social services, social workers will be at the mercy of contradictory pressures. On one hand, social workers are enjoined to do EBP, and, on the other, they do not have the time and resources to deepen their understanding of research relevant to their practice.

8

Policy Interventions against Urban Poverty

In the past few decades, urbanisation and urban growth have accelerated in many developing countries. In 1970, 37 percent of the world's population lived in cities. In 1995 this figure was 45 percent, and the proportion is expected to pass 50 percent by 2005. Urban populations are growing quickly—2.5 percent a year in Latin America and the Caribbean, 3.3 percent in Northern Africa, 4 percent for Asia and the Pacific and 5 percent in Africa. But, international comparisons are complicated by differing national definitions of urban areas. In Eastern Europe, Latin America and the Caribbean, the overall ratio of women to men is higher in urban areas than in rural areas, and the inverse is true for Africa and Asia.

Although in many third world cities natural population growth is the major contributor to urbanisation, rural-urban migration is still an important factor. Internal migration flows are diverse, complex and constantly changing. There is much diversity between nations and regions in terms of the age and level of education of migrants, and in the extent to which migration is considered permanent or temporary. A key determinant of migration is the income differential between rural and urban regions. Migration is also affected by crop prices, landowning structures and changes in agricultural technologies and crop mixes in surrounding areas and distant regions. It is also influenced by other factors related to individual or household structures and survival strategies, and wider political, economic and social forces.

There is no consensus on a definition of urban poverty but two broad complementary approaches are prevalent: economic and anthropological interpretations. Conventional economic definitions use incomeor consumption complemented by a range of other social indicators such as life expectancy, infant mortality, nutrition, the proportion of the household budget spent on food, literacy, school enrolment rates, access to health clinics or drinking water, to classify poor groups against a common index of material welfare. Alternative interpretations developed largely by rural anthropologists and social planners working with rural communities in the third world allow for local variation in the meaning of poverty, and expand the definition to encompass perceptions of non-material deprivation and social differentiation.

Anthropological studies of poverty have shown that people's own conceptions of disadvantage often differ from those of professional experts. Great value is attached to qualitative dimensions such as independence, security, self-respect, identity, close and non-exploitative social relationships, decision-making freedom and legal and political rights.

More generally, there has been a widening of the debates on poverty to include more subjective definitions such as vulnerability, entitlement and social exclusion. These concepts have been useful for analysing what increases the risk of poverty and the underlying reasons why people remain in poverty. Vulnerability is not synonymous with poverty, but refers to defencelessness, insecurity and exposure to risk, shocks and stress. Vulnerability is reduced by assets, such as: human investment in health and education; productive assets including houses and domestic equipment; access to community infrastructure; stores of money, jewellery and gold; and claims on other households, patrons, the government and international community for resources at times of need.

Entitlement refers to the complex ways in which individuals or households command resources which vary between people over time in response to shocks and long-term trends. Social exclusion is seen as a state of ill-being and disablement or disempowerment, inability which individuals and groups experience. It is manifest in 'patterns of social relationships in which individuals and groups are denied access to goods, services, activities and resources which are associated with citizenship'.

Most studies attempting to describe urban poverty have focused on drawing out the characteristics of urban poverty, often by comparing rural with urban poverty. However, there is still much debate as to whether urban poverty differs from rural poverty and whether policies to address the two should focus on different aspects of poverty.

In some views, rural and urban poverty are interrelated and there is a need to consider both urban and rural poverty together for they have many structural causes in common, e.g. socially constructed constraints to opportunities (class, gender) and macroeconomic policies (terms of trade). Many point to the important connections between the two, as household livelihood or survival strategies have both rural and urban components. Baker and Wratten illustrate this point in terms of rural-urban migration, seasonal labour, remittances and family support networks. Baker illustrates how urban and rural households adopt a range of diversification strategies, by having one foot in rural activities and another in urban. Conceptualising urban poverty as a separate category from rural poverty is also problematic because of different yardsticks for defining urban in different countries. The urban-rural divide is more a continuum rather than a rigid dichotomy.

Urban Development Policy

The rapid growth of urban populations has led to a worsening in absolute and relative poverty in urban areas. Urban poverty has, until recently, been low on the agenda of development policy because of dominant perceptions of urban bias and the need to counter this with a focus on rural development policy. However, policy interest in urban issues is increasing as a result of two phenomena:

- projections of a large and increasing proportion of poor people living in urban areas, partly as a result of urbanisation;
- and claims that structural adjustment programmes - which have removed some of the urban bias, by removing price distortions—have lead to a much faster increase in urban poverty than rural poverty.

There have been two broad traditions in policy approaches to urban poverty. The first set of approaches have focused on the physical infrastructure problems of housing, sanitation, water, land use and transportation. Recently there has been more emphasis on private investment and an increased focus on institutional and management aspects of urban development. The second set of broad approaches have focused on economic and social infrastructure issues such as employment, education and community services. Recently such approaches have put a lot of emphasis on sustainability issues and community involvement/participation in projects and programming.

More recently, concerns with the urban environment and violence and insecurity in urban areas have come to the fore as factors which undermine well-being and quality of life. There is some evidence of a strong relationship between poor health and poor environmental quality. The externalities of urban production are disproportionately borne by the poor because of the spatial juxtaposition of industrial and residential functions, high living densities, overcrowded housing in hazardous and inadequate supply of clean water, sanitation and solid waste disposal services.

Urban violence is estimated to have grown by between three and five percent a year over the last two decades, although there are large variations between nations and different cities within nations. Violent crimes are more visible in cities and there is growing understanding that violence should be considered a public health problem for which there are prevention strategies.

Urban violence is the result of many factors, and there is considerable debate about the relative importance of different factors. Certain specialists stress the significance of inadequate incomes which are usually combined with very poor and overcrowded housing and living conditions, and often insecure tenure, as fertile ground for development violence. Other explanations emphasise more the contemporary urban environment in which attractive goods are continuously on display and create targets for potential criminals. Oppression in all its forms, including the destruction of original cultural identities, together with racism are also cited as causes.

Gender, Poverty and Development

Gender issues have been increasingly discussed in the mainstream literature on urbanisation and urban poverty.

The urbanisation process is itself shaped by gender roles and relations. For instance the scale and nature of migration into urban areas in Latin America is much influenced by decisions in rural households about who should migrate and for what reason, by constraints placed on women's work outside the home by households, and by the demand for female labour in urban areas. Some studies have highlighted the extent to which migration patterns are differentiated by gender. These studies have shown that female migration is of much greater volume and complexity than was previously believed and that migration has gender-differentiated causes and consequences.

Female migration is increasing despite the constraints of women's dependent position within the family and society, as households are in need of income, and more employment opportunities are available to women. In some towns and cities in Latin America and the Caribbean, and parts of South East Asia, rural out-migration is female selective, urban sex ratios usually show more women than men and levels of female household headship are higher in urban than rural areas.

Nevertheless, in most of the developing world, single-male migration is more common. The effects of this on family structure, decision-making and women's autonomy and well-being are varied. Where family relations are strained by male absences and remittances are irregular or non-existent, it may lead to increased female poverty. On the other hand, households where women do receive remittances may be among the better off and gain independence and decision-making power through managing household resources.

Urbanisation tends to affect gender roles, relations and inequalities (although with great variety in the form and intensity from place to place) since the factors responsible for female-headed household (FHH) formation arise through urbanisation. This is evident in the transformation of household structures, the shifts in household survival strategies and changing patterns of employment.

There is a tendency to equate the growth in FHHs with the growth in poor or disadvantaged households- but female headship may have positive aspects. FHHs are likely to be less constrained by patriarchal authority at the domestic level and female heads may experience greater self-esteem, more personal freedom, more flexibility to take on paid work, enhanced control over finances and a reduction or absence of physical and/or emotional abuse. Female heads may be empowered in that they are more able to further their personal interests and the well-being of their dependants. Studies have shown that the expenditure patterns of female-headed households are more biased towards nutrition and education than those of male-households.

However, while female-headed households may be better off in some ways, they may still face discrimination, may face greater difficulties than men in gaining access to labour markets, credit, housing and basic services, and there are sometimes additional layers of discrimination against female heads. Single parent households, most of which are FHHs also face the difficulties of one adult having to combine income earning with household management and child rearing and this generally means that the parent can only take on part-time, informal jobs with low earnings and few if any fringe benefits.

There is limited consideration of gender issues with respect to measuring urban poverty, and identifying the urban poor. This has implications for the formation of policy and the design of antipoverty programmes. A review of current approaches to understanding urban poverty points to the need of broadening the way urban poverty is understood and measured. Official indicators of urban poverty often do not take into account gender-biased aspects of household impoverishment or coping strategies, such as limiting expenditure or resource use in times of economic crisis.

Conventional poverty lines give scant attention to health and social indicators, hence failing to demonstrate the social and health dimensions of urban poverty which are heavily borne by women. Consideration of urban poverty often neglects differentials between men and women in terms of their access to income, resources and services. Such differentials may occur within households between men and women or between individuals (i.e. between single men and single women) or between households with women-headed households at a disadvantage to male-headed households. There are also gender-based differentials in vulnerability to illness and violence.

A gender equality perspective draws attention to the need for gender-sensitive indicators of poverty. A way forward may be to develop indicators that measure gender-biased factors influencing the severity of poverty, such as capacity to achieve success, gender-differentiated needs, social and health dimensions of poverty etc.

Participatory approaches to measuring poverty may have more scope for including a gender analysis. Participatory poverty assessments which are broadly informed by a theory of social capital make visible the social norms and networks of supports of the poor, and highlight their capabilities, assets and resourcefulness. But they also need to be informed by frameworks which identify processes of social exclusion.

Feminist researchers have drawn attention to the fact that much of the literature on women, gender and urban development has fallen outside the mainstream. The realm of urban planning has been defined in physical and spatial terms, linked to men's work patterns, dealing with issues such as transport, housing, land and infrastructure whilst issues around health, education and the family, linked to women's work ,have been commonly dealt with as separate national level sectoral concerns.

In general, urban women's priorities have often been ignored in the design of human settlements, the location of housing, and the provision of urban services. However, there is increasing recognition of the discrimination faced by women in most aspects of employment, housing and basic services, and greater efforts by some governments and international agencies to reduce or remove this.

Gender equity considerations are important for any analysis of urban poverty conditions and trends. Men and women experience and respond to urban poverty in different ways as a result of gendered constraints and opportunities. There is gender-differentiated access to employment and income-earning opportunities in urban areas. Unemployment and underemployment have been major concerns for many urban economies. Recent studies suggest the urban poor have suffered significantly from structural adjustment through reduction in employment creation and downward pressure on real wages.

New categories of the poor have been identified, for example, former state employees who have been retrenched. In general terms, there are two broad labour market trends: the feminisation of the labour force; and the deregulation and casualistion of the labour market. The rise in female labour force participation can be attributed in part to a rise in demand for female labour in industries, and in part to household survival strategies during economic restructuring. This has positive benefits for women given that social position within, and access to, urban labour markets is critical for well-being and survival. However, there is evidence that in many countries gender segmentation in the labour market remains widespread and that women's work remains characterised by insecurity and low returns. Furthermore, many different facets of women's work, both unpaid and paid, are not recognised by urban planners.

Research on two low-income settlements in Madras, India suggests that neither household structure nor the structure of the economy can provide an adequate explanation of either female labour force participation or the type of work women and girls undertake in Madras. Ideological factors and their 'enforcement' at the intermediate social levels of the wider kingroup and community are central to decisions regarding who works in the household and under what conditions. These ideologies are, however, not rigid dictates but guiding principles around which the household respectability is negotiated.

The importance of the informal sector for income generation and poverty alleviation is well recognised. There is increasing reliance on urban informal employment for both men and women but the ability of the informal sector to absorb the unemployed is limited. There are genderdifferentiated patterns of access to informal sector work. Research in Zimbabwe revealed that declines in women's earnings from informal sector activities also meant less control by the women of household budgets, lower self esteem and increased conflict with husbands. Several of those interviewed felt that the men were not fulfilling their obligations as husbands and fathers.

The deregulation and casualisation of the labour market has lead to an increase in homeworking, particularly among women, which sometimes leads to greater exposure to environmental risk, both in terms of human pathogens and industrial toxic compounds at home or in the workplace.

Evidence from cities as diverse as Guayaquil, Harare, and Guadalajara indicate that with declining incomes and high unemployment, households have modified their consumption and dietary patterns and adjusted household expenditures, in many instances in the direction of cheaper and less nutritious substitutes. In Zimbabwe there is clear evidence that women have modified their lives to a greater extent than men. Women's responses were mainly individual, taking greater cuts in their own consumption, spending more time shopping for bargains and working longer hours for poorer returns.

The critical importance of assets and debt to the survival strategies of the poor in face of economic shocks has gender dimensions. Moser identifies the major assets of the poor in the face of economic crisis: labour; social and economic infrastructure; housing; household relations; social capital. In many instances, women have less command over assets than men.

An emerging area of concern is the increasing levels of crime and violence in urban areas. Important gender differentiation exists in terms of violent response to unemployment. While men turn to crime and violence, women more frequently turn to dependency on men. Research in Jamaica also points to important gender differences in terms of both involvement and impact of violence: economically motivated violence was seen primarily as involving men, while much of interpersonal violence involved women.

There is no conclusive evidence to suggest that gender-based violence is on the increase in urban areas. Some studies suggest that where it does occur, women have cited lack of money and food as the most important cause of marital conflict, and alcohol or drug abuse as the main reason for wife beating. They attributed men's anger to feelings of frustration stemming from insufficient earnings.

The determinants of health in urban areas are complex, but social and cultural factors, including composition of the family and cultural restrictions are important. Poor health can reduce capacity to earn an income, and health treatment can use up scarce savings or lead to debt. Women play a crucial role in informal health care in low-income households and communities in their role as wives and mothers, and continue to be used as conduits to children in promotional and preventative health campaigns, for example around nutrition and immunisation.

For South Asia as a whole it has been suggested that in the case of the urban poor, ill-health is the most important trigger pushing households into poverty and destitution, particularly when the person sick is the adult wage earner is male. This raises questions as to who in a household gets access to health care when user charges are imposed. This may disadvantage girls and women and privilege boys and men in low-income households.

Indoor air pollution and airborne lead have been identified as among the most serious pollution problems in developing countries. Women and children spend more time at home than men do, are more exposed to indoor pollution, and hardest hit by respiratory disease. Although women are more exposed to air pollution from household fuels and to contaminated water, there has been little research on the different health consequences of pollution for women and men.

Men and women play different roles in the environmental management in cities. Research in Latin America indicates that poor women are more likely than men to undertake the majority of environmental management tasks such as purification of water and management of domestic waste.

Lack of access to secure and safe housing is a central feature of urban poverty. At least 600 million urban dwellers in Africa, Asia and Latin America live in housing that is so overcrowded and of such poor quality, with such inadequate provision for water, sanitation, drainage and garbage collection that their lives and their health is continually at risk (UNCHS). Housing is also an important productive asset since access to credit to secure a livelihood may depend on property ownership. The price and availability of land for housing remains an important influence on housing prices and conditions leading to the development of illegal or informal land markets, where the poor have limited capacity to pay. Quantity, quality, accessibility and tenure of housing are all important and have gender-specific dimensions.

There is increased awareness of possible 'gender blindness' in housing and basic service programmes, because they do not recognise and make provision for the particular needs and priorities of women for income-earning, child-rearing and household management, and communitylevel action and management. Low-cost housing or site and service programmes rarely consider the needs and priorities of women in terms of site design and nature of infrastructure and service provision that meet their needs. The ways and means in which discrimination takes place is well documented, i.e. exclusion of women through eligibility criteria, methods of beneficiary recruitment, cost recovery mechanisms. There are also gender dimensions to renting and gender-related constraints to owner-occupation. Studies of Latin

America and West Africa suggest that female-headed households are more likely to be tenants or sharers than owners, whilst a study in Bangladesh found that female-headed households and supported households were concentrated in the poorest and potentially most vulnerable housing conditions. There are several reasons for this:

— women are often excluded from official housing programmes offering owner occupation;

— female-headed households tend to be poorer and, since poorer households frequently rent, women tend to be tenants;

— female-headed households also frequently lack both time and skills to self-build, but are often required to do so in the absence of funds for professional labour.

However, the tendency to portray women as victims is questionable in light of women's involvement in low-income housing as landlords and illegal developers of urban land. Research on Mexican cities highlights women's direct role in self-help housing construction directly, and their crucial role in underpinning the social relations on which much of the mutually supportive activity of self-help housing construction rests.

There has been a decline in investment in urban infrastructure such as transport, sanitation, and water provision in many developing country cities. Official statistics suggest that by the early 1990s more than 80 percent of the urban population in Africa, Asia and Latin America were 'adequately served' with water, at least a third have no proper sanitation, and three-fifths were not connected to a public sewerage system. Governments tend to exaggerate the proportion of people with piped water, and there is much disagreement about the definition of 'adequate'. Inadequate supply of water and sanitation facilities may place time constraints on women, as they are more likely to have the responsibility for tasks that require water. When planning transport there is no consideration of the fact that women also have to perform reproductive tasks. Women may be severely disadvantaged by the fact that transport often runs infrequently during off-peak periods.

Gender-based Policy Interventions

There are relatively few examples given of successful anti-poverty policies in urban areas in the development literature. This may be attributed to the fact that most of the work on urban issues has been carried out by geographers, receiving less attention from economists. The increasing sociological and anthropological work on urban issues particularly in Latin America may bring about some change.

One area of urban anti-poverty policy that has witnessed much theoretical and empirical work, and considerable success in benefiting the poor is slum improvement and basic services provision. But even such initiatives have tended to be biased towards the non-poor.

A significant change during the 1980s and 1990s is the shift from housing needs to housing rights as a result of increasing influence on government actions of international and national law on people's right to housing, largely as a result of much greater use of international and national law by NGOs. Various new approaches to settlements planning and management have been developed over the last 10-15 years in the form of settlement planning, land use control (improved zoning techniques, innovations in land development and management), the management of infrastructure (management of environmental infrastructure, financing investments, paying for water) and transport planning and management.

In recent years there have been initiatives to reduce discrimination and ensure a greater voice and influence for women's needs and priorities in housing, and more generally human settlements. However, the tendency has been to focus on women's need for income generation rather than their housing needs. It is now more common to find discussions of women's livelihood and housing needs together. Some credit programmes that developed for income generation have also developed credit programmes for housing purchase, construction and improvement, e.g. the Grameen Bank.

Increasing attention is being given to urban employment creation. The new emphasis on selfemployment promotion corresponds with changing views on the informal sector. There is also much interest in microenterprise sector development in the context of priorities emerging in liberalising economies such as developing the private sector, creating employment, alleviating poverty and encouraging more equitable income distribution.

The health sector, perhaps more than any other, targets women in urban areas. But this has not always meant it has addressed women's health needs and rights. Health care remains highly medicalised and professionalised, and poor men and women continue to be excluded from formal or public health care. Cost recovery approaches to financing health services have gendered implications for affordability.

A gendered approach which addresses simultaneously and equitably the different preventative and curative health needs of both men and women is required. The limitations of supply based, top down responses has led to various conclusions about what may improve urban conditions. The failure of large scale infrastructure based projects to provide sustainable action has been interpreted in different ways. A range of alternative approaches have been taken particularly by NGOs:

— institutional support; greater use of low cost technology in infrastructure responses;

— integrated programmes of health, education, shelter and infrastructure support; basic needs support targeted at the poor;

— radical programmes based on community needs and community involvement; involving NGOs more in these community based responses, as an alternative to government/municipality agencies support.

The role of women at grassroots or community level is also becoming better appreciated by external agencies. Several case studies suggest that community organisations in which women have a major role are more effective than those controlled by men, e.g. the Integrated Slum Improvement Programme in Visakhpatnam; it is in the few examples of settlements that are led by women that the rhetoric of urban community development has most closely been translated into reality. There are examples of women's housing projects, or housing projects that address the particular needs of women or women-headed households.

Community activism is an important avenue towards participation in city-level planning and policy making processes. But, there is the danger that if women confine themselves to organising self-help and survival strategies they will be left to manage communities on their own, without resources or political and professional support.

Recent concern with urban governance stems from general attention being paid to the issue of 'good governance' in development. It is essentially preoccupied with questions of financial accountability and administrative efficiency, and political concerns related to democracy, human rights, and participation. Urban governance used to be equated solely with urban management but more recently, it has come to be understood both as government responsibility and civic engagement involving a full range of participants, which makes it more possible to integrate a gender perspective. Women need to participate in public office because they have particular experiences of, and relationships to, the urban environment, and they have proved themselves to be effective agents of change at the city or local level on a range of issues.

Poverty analysis must focus on a household's means of survival and its room for manoeuvre in adopting different coping strategies. This necessarily involves a discussion of household composition and gender relations. Such an analysis must go beyond a solely income-based view of poverty and include an understanding of vulnerability, entitlement and social exclusion which emphasises the importance of assets and processes of exclusion.

The role of governance, institutions and partnerships with individuals, households, communities, voluntary organisation, NGOs, private enterprises, investors and government agencies is continuously emphasised in the urban development literature. There is a need to develop gendersensitive mechanisms and ways to involve both men and women in the processes of identifying needs and planning. To address the scale and complex nature of urban poverty problems, national and local capacity building institutions will need to be strengthened, ensuring that training is in local languages, gender-sensitive and involves all actors.

New forms of urban partnership are required to develop participatory processes that include women and men at all stages of urban development. Participation as entitlement refers to how women and men command resources, contribute to, and take responsibility for the well-being of their households, communities and the city. Participation as empowerment relates to processes by which organised groups in cities identify and articulate their interests, negotiate change with others, and transform urban organisation life and their role within it. More research is required on women, citizenship, democratisation and decentralisation and its relationship with urban governance.

9

Social Work and Community Policing

The new philosophies community policing and problem oriented policing have started a lot of discussion across the world. This is mostly due to the fact that the results of these new strategies sound very promising.It seems to be rather easy to transfer these philosophies and insights of community and problem oriented policing results to countries in which law enforcement and criminal justice administration are guided by the so-called opportunity principle.

Under the opportunity principle it is in general agencies officially allowed or they are even entitled by law to abandon any persecution, to dismiss a case formally, to enter an alternative way of dealing with the case, or to charge the culprit eventually with a lesser offence than that originally prosecuted. In some of the States this discretionary power is even more or less completely given to the police authorities or individual police officers on the beat. On the contrary will countries, in which law enforcement agencies and criminal justice administrations are guided by the so-called legality principle, face many difficulties when trying to introduce community- or problem oriented policing. These philosophies and practices aim at improving the relationship between the authorities, the citizens, and the communities. This relationship implies the development of social-psychological bonds based on mutual exchange relations and trustworthiness between the police and the citizens. This relationship is supposed in the long run to improve the quality of life in the community and to make the living conditions for the people more secure. The legality principle stays in stark contrast with those goals and principles. It requires, when strictly administered, that every agent of the law enforcement agencies and the administration of criminal justice treats every case formally and officially and has no discretion whatsoever. Whenever there is suspicion that a crime may have been committed these persons have to start an official procedure, to record the already known details of the case, to start an investigation, and to charge the suspect eventually with the relevant counts before a criminal court.

Nowadays, nearly no system adhering to the legality principle, like Germany, Austria or Switzerland, does administer it in practice in the traditional strict way anymore. There were partly official laws introducing exceptions, partly leeway opened by court decisions or by guidelines. This development gave prosecutors and judges a couple'practitioners of new possibilities to deal with cases and suspects in a discretionary manner. But the police were as a rule not entitled to act likewise. They have, for example in Germany, no legal power to decide by themselves on how to proceed a case. Quite contrary are the police officers required to take note of every case, and to report it to the public prosecutor by adding all the existing files and evidence. Only very minor traffic transgressions are excepted, for instance parking violations, where the police officer on the beat has some discretion whether to give only an immediate oral warning, to write a ticket or to enter a special procedure to be handled further by the traffic authority.

Even though the police in Germany have in the field of order maintenance and the safeguarding of public life the usual discretionary power, one has to conclude that the theories of community policing and problem oriented policing may be doomed to fail in countries with the legality principle. In many everyday situations the aspects of law enforcement and order maintenance are intrinsically intertwined. In some circumstances police officers get complaints about events that formally fulfil all the legal requirements of a criminal offence but are negligible in substance. There may typically exist no need for law enforce-ment, but only some friendly, direct advice and perhaps immediate restitution or reconciliation. Under the legality principle the police officer has only a bad choice: if he does not act formally, he runs the risk of getting charged himself in case his decision is being reported to the prosecutors office.

The implementation of these new policing philosophies would not be possible without a substantial modification or the abandonment of the legality principle. The modifications or the abandonment would allow that the concepts of community- and problem oriented policing could be implemented in Germany, Austria, and Switzerland, improve life for its citizens and fulfil the wishes and expectations of the citizens toward their police.

Development of Community Policing

The traditional style of policing was to keep public peace and order, to enforce laws, making arrests, and to provide short-term solutions to occurring problems. This concept stood in contrast to the policing style proposed by Sir Robert Peel for a professional police force in Great Britain which was passed by the British Parliament in 1829 and which stressed the preventive nature of the new law: "... the principal object to be attained is the prevention of crime. The security of persons and property will thus be better effected, than by the detection and punishment of the offender after he has succeeded in committing the crime".

The principles of Peel's proposed policing can again be found since the early 1980's when community policing emerged as the dominant direction for new ways in thinking about policing. Parallel to the reintroduction of the concept of community policing developed Goldstein 1979 and later Eck and Spelman 1987 the concept of problem oriented policing.

Even though these two concepts, community policing and problem oriented policing, are analytically separate and distinct, argue Peak and Glensor convincingly that they are complementary in substance, and can be operated together. Peak and Glensor coined the term "community oriented policing and problem solving" (COPPS) in which they try to integrate the two concepts. One welfare and their'important aspect so far is the communities' and the citizens working together with the police. This is well in line with an argument already put forward by Sir Peel: "The police are only members of the public who are paid to give fulltime attention to duties which are incumbent on every citizen in the interest of the community welfare". One may ask, however, whether at all, and how well this cooperation between communities and the police works in modern, industrialised and socially more or less fragmented societies.

A possible way to measure this question seems to ask citizens about their attitudes towards, and their experiences with, the police. Survey results and other material pertaining fully and specifically to community policing and problem oriented policing are seemingly nonexistent. In this chapter we take therefore a rather broad view. We will consider how the public views and perceives the police and their work in general, what the expectations of the citizens are towards the police, and how actual policing levels of fear of'styles or manners are affecting the citizens crime and feelings of insecurity in their neighbourhoods.

Based on the assumption that in today world the working together between the police and the citizens is almost nonexistent, was the concept of community policing developed in the early 1980's. Among the reasons for the rather loose, sometimes tense or even bad relationship between the police and the community were a lack of trust in and scepticism about the police. This was partly due to the fact that in the past in many regions, cities, places etc. close personal contacts between the police authorities or individual police officers and the citizens, apart from the handling of concrete events, were generally rather scarce.

However, in order to get background knowledge about the typical characteristics of the population and their living environment, which was seen as essential to reach an improved crime clearance rate and to better prevent future crimes, a close relationship and good everyday cooperation between the police and the community members seemed absolutely necessary. Therefore the concept of community policing aims to reunite the police with, respectively to immerse them into the community. It is a holistic concept, definitely surpassing technocratic solutions as liked by bureaucratic apparatusses.

We can summarise the principles of community policing as following:

— Community policing is based on the assumption that there is no real distinction between the substantive function of policing between members of the general public and particular office-holders. To put it in a slogan: police are the public and the public are the police. That means that the police officers are just those who are paid to give fulltime attention to the duties of every citizen.

- Community policing is based upon commitment for far reaching, broad problem oriented service. It is much more than just an addition to the traditional event oriented policing style.
- Community policing is based upon an organisational decentralisation and on the reconstruction of police work in favour of a two-way-communication between the police and the citizens.
- Community policing requests that the police, representing but one department among many others responsible for improving the quality of life, respond towards the wishes of the citizens and, even in the absence of crime and disorder, to whatever problems disturb the community most.
- The police and their work serve as a catalyst to organise the community and to enhance public cooperation amongst the citizens.
- The attention on community policing concentrates it signs of disorder or incivility such as vandalism, graffiti, abandoned housing, trash, etc.
- Community policing favours foot patrols by the police which allows the police officer to experientally "learn his beat".
- Community policing supports the idea that local police officers function as "problem brokers" and coordinate the communication with (other) public institutions and the members and associations of the community.
- Community policing implies a special cooperation between the police and the citizens for crime

prevention. Recurring problems are supposed to be solved by going back over and over to the same places in order to evaluate the efforts of both sides.

— Community policing tries to involve every citizen of a whole community in the activities to reduce and control acute crime problems, drug markets, fear of crime, the decline of the neighbourhood in order to improve the quality of life in the community.

— Community policing is based upon the idea that the activities of the police have to be extended in the communities to become an institution that cares and coordinates efforts to improve social cohesion, if and at times where a diffusion of the community takes place and ties among organisations and citizens of a community become weaker. Crime control in general and combatting acute particular crimes remain still important aspects of policing in everyday practice. But s main focus on keeping the public peaceful, on'community policing has it mediating conflicts, and on coordinating efforts to improve the whole quality of life in the community.

Problem Oriented Policing

The police authorities have always tried, in addition to clearing up reported criminal incidents and to chasing suspected offenders, to solve problems occuring in their jurisdiction. Individual police officers took always care of problems they were faced with in their beat while on duty. But the concept of what a police problem is all about was rather limited and, in a certain way, typologically concretistic.

Keeping public peace and order, clearing a difficult or even dangerous traffic situation, providing first service in cases of personal emergency, effecting first measures and alarming other authorities like the fire brigade, helping people and animals out of acute trouble, providing guidance for persons in need of care, offering advise for precautionary measures with regard to crime prevention: this is but a selection of what a responsive and responseful police authority or representative may have done and still will do in their regular work. This is not to be contested. However, problems of that type are probably mere surface phenomena.

Seen from the point of view of community policing they may emerge out of deeper seated, more far reaching if not structural problems affecting the whole social space and the social-psychological web of a neighbourhood, a small village, a little town or a certain region of a city or metropolitan area. In the past there existed no guidance or a concept on how to detect and tackle such problems in a community.

The philosophy of problem solving policing aims to improve exactly that situation. It was developed by Goldstein in 1979 out of frustration with the dominant, i.e. more technological if not technocratic model for improving police operations. At the time the police in the U.S. and in many other Western industrialised countries were much more concerned e.g. about how quick they were in responding to a call than in asking what may have caused the fact that the concrete call was the 55th arriving from that locality within the last three months .Accordingly it was important for them to look for the necessary evidence for immediate law enforcement and eventual criminal justice procedures, but it didn't matter that much what they did otherwise with persons or situations affected by the event once they arrived at the scene of a crime.

The police administrations lacked a concept which offered the police officers ways and means to detect signs of problems behind the manifested problem, and particular techniques to address such problems if detected on the occasion or in the aftermath of the event. Problem oriented policing tries to develop such concepts. It has so far a strong community inclination. In accordance with Peak and Glensor one can therefore conclude that problem oriented policing relates to different principles than community oriented policing, but that both are complementary.

Problem oriented policing may thus be perceived as a strategy that puts the community oriented policing philosophy into practice. The police as organisation is supposed to look for and to examine the underlying causes of emerging crimes and disorders, and to find long term solutions. When grasping the essence of the concept of problem solving policing every individual police officer should feel enabled to contribute to the continuous task of identifying problems, analysing them rigorously, developing strategies to moderate or even eliminate them, and later to evaluate the outcome.

According to Goldstein problem oriented policing means an encompassing plan to improve the work of the police by focusing their attention on the most serious background factors which have far reaching consequences for all levels of the structure and the organisation of their duties. Goldstein argues further that the usual police behaviours are oriented towards the wrong categories. Not a crime category such as murder should e.g. be decisive on what kind of facts the energy should be directed at and the methods should be applied. The police have instead to evaluate and search for the objective causes and subjective reasons (motives etc.) behind the open or at least easily tangible crime scene, and to develop proactive and long term problem solving concepts for an area of social conflict. This does not imply, of course, that a local police authority with a high incidence of homicide cases could or should undo a standing and suitably equipped homicide squad or department.

Crimes that happen have always to be dealt with in terms of clearance and appropriate law enforcement. The guiding idea is rather pointing at a meta-level of everyday work. According to that idea the police work may just start on the surface of an event since that is often the way the responsible persons gain knowledge of what happens out there. Sometimes already a single event can be significant for what basically determines the trouble people and/or localities are suffering from.

At least repeated events or continuous nuisances should make the police alert to look for other than the evident contingencies of the situation. They are supposed to pursue the contextual elements of crime in the community, beyond the concrete cases and independent of the traditional detective tasks and endeavours. To put it in more classical criminological terms: they are expected to tackle the root causes of crime in a given environment, and not just to deal with the surface of singular crimes or series of offences originating there by the one or the other coincidence of different circumstances.

Consequently should individual police officers not restrain themselves to think about single case solutions but rather strive to contribute to the development of complete societal problem solution strategies. The latter should then trickle down in the organisation, structure, and the training of the whole police corps, in particular with regard to sensitise new recruits and to hold alert already s why Torstensson called'qualified experienced officers.

Several steps must be taken in order to improve the quality of police responses. Eck and Spelman seem to offer a suitable concept so far. They developed a twelve step model of what a problem oriented policing agency should do:

1. Focus on problems of concern to the public.
2. Zero in on effectiveness as the primary concern.
3. Be proactive.
4. Be committed to systematic inquiry as a first step in solving substantive problems.
5. Encourage the use of rigorous methods in making inquiries,
6. Make full use of the data in police files and the experience of police personnel.
7. Group like incidents together so that they can be addressed as a common problem.
8. Avoid using overly broad labels in grouping incidents so separate problems can be identified.
9. Encourage a broad and uninhibited search for solutions.
10. Acknowledge the limits of the criminal justice system as a response to problems.
11. Identify multiple interests in any one problem and weigh them when analysing the value of different responses.
12. Be committed to taking some risks in responding to problems.

Problem Oriented vs. Community Policing

Police experts were looking for two decades for alternative ways to reduce the steady increasing crime rates and to combat crime through preventive measures. Problem oriented policing and community policing have both the same philosophical roots and share according to Moore and Trojanowicz some important characteristics:

1. decentralisation in order to encourage officer initiative and the effective use of local knowledge.

2. geographical rather than functionally defined subordinate units in order to develop local knowledge.
3. close interactions with local communities in order to facilitate responsiveness to, and cooperation with, the community.

Problem oriented policing mainly tries to solve regional crime problems, however, the main focus is the solving of crimes and the underlying causes of the crime through restructuring of the police force and changes in the police organisation. The main focus of community oriented policing is on the other hand the improvement of the relationship between the police and the citizens.

Both concepts overlap in the area where problem oriented policing is depending on information of the citizens and a good relationship with the community. Further on in areas where potential conflict in the population leads to conflicts which problem oriented policing wants to solve, such conflicts would not have occurred through community policing. Each community oriented police work includes problem solving strategies, but the complete problem oriented police work is not necessarily community oriented. Problem oriented policing does not necessarily include long term evaluations in order to guarantee that the solutions to the problems will be long lasting. The interventions through problem oriented policing can change the structure of the community, they are, however, limited since the police are coming into the community, make changes and disappear. This does not apply for community oriented policing since in this case the police come into the neighbourhood/community, stays there and take on the responsibility to improve the quality of communal life.

Peak and Glensor engage, as already mentioned above, in conceiving of an integrated model called community oriented policing and problem solving (COPPS). They describe the essence of their concept as follows:

> "Community oriented policing and problem solving is a proactive philosophy that promotes solving problems that are criminal, affect our quality of life, or increase our fear of crime, as well as relate to other community issues. COPPS encourages using various resources and police-community partnerships for developing strategies to identify, analyse, and address community problems at their source".

Problem-oriented Policing and Citizens

The question is now how those ideas are related to the subjective world of the citizenry. Do people accept the philosophy? Would the citizens be prepared to have the police integrated into their interpersonal and communal affairs? How would this affect their attitudes towards the police forces in general, since there are a couple of other policing authorities in modern states than just the particular local one? Would the eventual positive attitude toward problem oriented policing lead to a lasting cooperation with police officers and institutions? Is it foreseeable that all, the majority or at least a substantial and evenly distributed minority of the community members will feel instigated to engage in further improving the local social fabric. Will the citizens do this in a constant and wise manner and enhance the basic quality of life for all residents? What do people expect the new police to be like? What kind of views do the citizens have with regard to the new definition of the situation?

We were up to date not able to find any study addressing those and other related questions in a specific and coherent way. It seems therefore that the criminology, criminal justice and police research community has hitherto rather speculated on behalf of the people instead of asking them directly. There exist data, however, explicating one or the other aspect of attitudes toward, expectations of, and experiences with the police in'citizens other contexts, but not explicitly to test if problem solving policing would be accepted by the citizens. Perhaps scholars relied in a more global an indirect manner on relevant results when they developed and worked on their models of problem and community oriented policing. We decided, however, to refrain from 'further refining conceptual issues and to take views of citizens and citizens expectations of problem solving policing as an empirical issue.

Sometimes the original data show a close connection to questions of problem oriented or community policing, and can therefore easily be interpreted within our framework of thinking. Sometimes we have to try harder to make new sense out of original results. Data have to be recoded or regrouped before they fit into the different concept of our analysis. The reinterpretation of results collected s own is' under a certain theoretical perspective different from one' always a risky endeavour.

There is one common theme of problem oriented policing and community policing. Both stress the fact that the relationship between the police and the community/ citizens are of utmost importance. In the eyes of the American citizens is the most important duty of the police to protect and serve. However, what the citizens exactly want from their police force and how they view their duties and obligations seems quite ambivalent. In general citizens favour a strong police force. However, they often do not report crimes to the police, and if they do, the level of their satisfaction with the police varies and is generally not extraordinary high. We will in a first step examine how much confidence the German citizens have in their public institutions and among them in the police.

There exist substantial differences between the old and new States of the Federal Republic of Germany. The confidence in nearly all public institutions is in the old States much higher than in the new States. In the old States we find only in 1992 and 1993 that the citizens viewed the parties negatively. The constitutional court was ranked highest in the old States as well as in the new States, even though in the latter the level of confidence was somewhat lower as compared to the old States. Courts were ranked very high in the old States and with the exception of 1991 fairly high in the new States.

The police in the old States received a ranking on the second or the third position. That means that the West German citizens show a high and rather stable level of confidence in police but, in the long range, trust is slowly but steadily decreasing since 1984. East German citizens answered in quite a different way. In the first survey that included the new States the average result was negative. No other German survey had ever produced negative police rankings. Results did not even come near to zero. So this particular result can be taken as sign for deep seated distrust in that type of government agency normally representing, to speak with Max Weber, the monopoly of legitimate force of the State.

The comparatively low confidence in the police s police'can be explained by the past experience of the citizens with the people in the former German Democratic Republic. It seems that the distance to, if not the contempt of the all-intruding State Secret Service heavily influenced the attitudes of the citizens towards the police. The so-called Stasi was organised as a distinct and separate department of the central government like, for example, the Department of Justice or the Department of Agriculture.

The Stasi had central, regional, and local offices and under certain circumstances additional specialised offices.

The Stasi was therefore not part of the regular police forces but had, inter alia, the power to interfere with police operations, to give them directions, or to take over a case. It was, by the same token, the strong arm of the leading party, the Unified Socialist Party of Germany that owned the state in political terms.

So the Volkspolizei was in many ways dependent on the Stasi and on the dominating party politics. After the German unification the police force in the new States was completely restructured and built up new along the Western democratic model. But it obviously took a while in this process to deal effectively with the shadows of the past. On the one hand the citizens had after the unification a very high level of insecurity and expressed a need for a strong police force, but on the other hand they could not easily overcome their generalised distrust in any kind of police force given their experience with the repressive aspects of the old regime. The ranking is improving now rather quickly. Murck found also in his study that the citizens of the new States developed a much better relationship with their new police rather quickly. 22% of the interviewed citizens in his study reported that the relationship towards the police is much friendlier, 58% reported that it is slightly better and only 16% reported that the relationship did not improve at all. It is interesting that males from the East had the highest percentage of very negative or at least fairly negative attitudes towards the police while the women in the new States exhibited a far more positive orientation.

In East Germany governed a social insecurity due to the need of reorientation and restruction of the social system. This insecurity is not only- as described above - being realised by the East German population, but also brings about a change in the polices jobhandling and shows up in the realisation of personal interests and needs.

In 1991 Rafael Behr studied a police department in the new federal states for several weeks. He made the following observations: Most police officers felt personally burdened especially due to the increase of robberies and bank robberies, a fact which barely existed in the former GDR. They were also more frequently exposed to life threatening situations, the perpetrators were more brutal and using weapons, circumstances they were not used to. Therefore the police officers felt no longer that the criminals "inferior" to the police. In earlier times there was no need for the use of weapons; this was regulated by the government and MFS-apparatus. The police officers showed great fear of being victimised themselves. Furthermore Behr found that the relationship of the East Germans police with the population was after the unification most problematic. Most contacts between police and the population appear in cases where citizens ask for their help. However, the traditional East German police force barely sought contact towards the citizens. There was a tendency to regulate state affairs quickly and there was no understanding of long discussions with the citizens leaving alone the fact to involve them in police matters. It is in this context interesting that the absolute number of contacts between East German police and the population is far lower than in West Germany. Behr talks about an `informal control moratorium' of the East German police. Behr mentions several reasons for the small amount of contacts initiated by the police. Next to insufficient technical equipment, there exists an unconscious fear to provoke feelings or remarks made by citizens who would treat the contact to the police as a form of control and which reminded them of the unpleasant relationship between them, the police and the former Stasi.

All together, the East German police makes an insecure appearance toward the population. The reason for it is found in their vulnerability due to their collective and not their personal past. Therefore they tend to avoid any contact to the population, which goes beyond the necessary measures and the police forces in the five new States will have to come an even longer way as the counterparts in the old States to incorporate the principles of community and problem oriented policing. The same is true for the citizens in the new States of Germany which have to learn that the police can be trusted and can be a "friend and helper".

The citizens of Germany call generally for a strong police. This call increased over time and goes hand in hand with experiencing more problems in general and greater feelings of insecurity in society. The extent of the wish to be guarded by a strong police force is much more pronounced in the new States of the united Germany. Accordingly the call for a strong police force is substantially higher compared to the old States of Germany which indicates a higher level of subjective insecurity in the new States. Asked whether the police are very important for the protection of the citizen answered in 1991 49% of the citizens in the old States and 63% of the citizens in the new States of Germany accordingly, while only 5% in the West and 2% in the East reported that the police are not important at all.

The German population tends to have positive attitudes towards their police in general. This was aptly shown in the past, for example by Stephan in his Stuttgart survey. Around 96% of the citizens of that city with a population of 600.000 thought that their police had a good reputation and police men/woman were decent people. 95% thought that police officers were friendly people and 87% of the inhabitants found that they should be more honoured. Kerner conducted in 1976 a study on the state of domestic security in Germany. A representative sample of (West) German citizens and a quota sample of young police officers were questioned about a couple of problems regarding the structure and development of crime, relations.

The police survey allowed'fear of crime, and police-citizens additional questions for the latter aspect. When asked whether they feared to get into trouble with the police 65% of the population answered with not at all, and an additional 19% with rather seldom. However, it is interesting to note that the police officers were more sceptical in that s'respect. Kerner asked them about their heterostereotype of people expectations: 63% of them thought that the general population would expect trouble with the police. Asked about their own fear to get confronted with citizens 18% of the police officers responded with constantly or often, and an additional 29% with at least sometimes. The officers opinions may have reflected their tendency to generalise from single, but nevertheless repeated problematic encounters with normal people in public. Therefore they tended to consider themselves more friendly towards the citizens than they believe these would be willing to recognise. In the 70ies the public relations slogan "The police, your friends and helpers" was quite popular and often utilised, inter alia, in newspaper ads. The police officers liked this slogan: 83% reported that the advertisement was completely or mostly correct. But they expected that only 49% of the normal population would consent to this statement as well. In addition believed the police officers that 18% of the population would think it is completely true and 50% that it is rather true that people are happy when not seeing and not hearing the police at all.

The question is how far this ambivalence and distance on the part of the population as indicated in police heterostereotyping reflect the true opinion of the people. For those basic attitudes would probably hamper, inter alia, the development of effective problem and community oriented policing schemes. We do not have adaequate data to answer the question directly. When trying to find evidence that allows at least indirect conclusions one can, in our opinion, partly rely on victimisation studies in so far as these studies crime incident reporting behaviour.

The latest German study was'analyse victims done by Heinz and Spiess in the twin-city Ravensburg/ Weingarten in South-Western Germany. They looked at the reasons why citizens did not report their victimisations to the police. Around 70% of the victims did not report the crimes to the police, which stands in great contrast to the above mentioned findings that the citizens in Germany are in favour of a strong police force. Their results imply more a kind of reduced expectation of citizens toward the police than a real distance.

Slightly over 50 percent of the citizens who became the victim of a crime did not report the event to the police since they thought the police couldn't have done anything about it or there was not enough objective evidence for the commitment of a crime. In addition reported 47 percent of the citizens that the committed crimes were not serious enough to be reported, or that no damage occurred. These results indicate that around half of the citizens do not consider their victimisations as serious enough to outweight the endeavours of reporting them to the police. Besides these facts show citizens a very pragmatic and realistic adjustment towards their victimisation by stating that the police would not have done anything. Of particular interest is that 85.1 percent of the citizens who were victimised by a aggravated or simple assault did not report these crimes to the police.

There seems to be an ambivalence in the opinions of the people about, and their satisfaction with the police in general. This picture is further supported by a look at the level of satisfaction especially with the police performance. People appear not to expect too much in terms of police efficiency and effectiveness. The police are considered to be necessary agents of control in modern societies. They are therefore accepted as part of the social fabric. Since every form of social control bears both aspects, helping and restricting, seemingly contradictory opinions may actually not contradict each other but rather complement each other.

Good citizens just happen to make errors sometimes or they can not always avoid to bypass the laws and have to ask regulations which are too strict anyway: Therefore the police don for a formalistic way of law abidance, they have instead to show flexibility and indulgence. Those considerations may eventually lead to an integrated set of mixed feelings toward the police among the people. Generally positive attitudes may prevail even if one does not really like police authorities in a given situation of State and society, since one may be well aware that all other social institutions or agencies will provide even less help and emergency assistance than the police will normally do. General positive attitudes on the societal level allow further critical attitudes to-wards the local police and vice versa. There seems to be a proximity effect in that the evaluation of local conditions is more open to experiential influences out of direct police-citizen contacts and out of indirect knowledge experiences and from community gossip. We' or friends'stemming from relatives can approach the tendencies of these questions partly by looking at recent surveys.

In the German study people were asked to evaluate'In Kerner police efficiency in their immediate neighbourhood. Only 17% were mostly or fully discontent whereas 82% showed different levels of satisfaction. It is interesting to note that the police officers came quite close in their estimate of what the population thinks of local policing; they had, however, a slightly more negative direction in their answers: 12% of the officers thought residents to be mostly or fully discontent whereas 73% assumed they would be satisfied (39% partly content, 33% mostly content, 1% completely content); around 10% did not dare to take a clear position. In a more recent study in Unna, Germany, an industrial town in the Rhein-Ruhr-region of Germany, citizens were asked in which way they wanted to improve the work of the police. The answers can be interpreted to a certain extent as expression of satisfaction vs. dissatisfaction with local policing.

When the citizens were asked if the control through the police should be increased, they tended to the notion that they do not want to see the police in all areas with potential interference of policing with their own habitat or routine activities. The number of citizens who were in favour of more radar control, more traffic control, and more drunk driver testing were fairly low. This result fits very well into what Kerner attitudes is concerned:'found in 1976 as police heterostereotype of peoples Only 6% of the officers said that the German population would prefer the police 'to enforce traffic laws; however, the top issue was guaranteeing peoples security. When asked "In what respect do you think that the population feels the police control too much?" around 76% ranked traffic law enforcement first.

The police as law enforcers are esteemed in as much they control and catch the so-called true criminals, and the German police officers were well aware of this basic attitude: around 88% thought the people would like them to enforce the law and only 3% meant they were considered to be too harsh. The criminals are more or less out there or at least the others for the standard population.

As a consequence the law abiding citizens, need not real control but rather advise, care, and help. Given this type of attitude one would expect that people condone or even seek all forms of policing representing the promise of good public order and peace. So far the public seems also basically be in favour of the positive issues built into concepts of community and problem oriented policing.

The inhabitants of Unna can be taken as an example: they favoured to a high degree policing measures such as more talking with the citizens, more police counselling and more cooperation with other authorities/institutions. They consequently did not so much vote for increasing the patrols by bikes and cars, but preferred to see more pedestrian patrols by the police. This survey clearly indicates that the citizens like to perceive the police as friends and helpers and they would support endeavours to improve the work of the police force much in the sense of what community and problem oriented policing propose.

A further assessment of the quality of the local police work can be found in the study by Heinz and Spiess for the cities of Ravensburg and Weingarten. The citizens were asked to evaluate the police on a grade scale of one to six. The city inhabitants were, with a grade point average of 3.1. fairly satisfied with the current work of the police in their community. This grade is slightly lower then the one for the Federal Republic of Germany which may be due to the above mentioned proximity effect. The younger age groups scored the lowest and were not so satisfied with the work of the police. On the other hand were those citizens who had just recently seen a police patrol in their neighbourhood much more content with the police work than any other group. Victims and nonvictims among the citizens assessed the police work not structurally different but, however, a negative effect seemed to emanate from multiple victimisations. While the difference between one time victims and nonvictims is rather small assess multiple victims the work of the police quite negative.

Fear of crime is a very important measure on how well the citizens feel in their neighbourhood and how high is the quality of life. In the latest survey in Germany about the "anxieties of the nation" the Germans ranked fear of crime after unemployment as the second highest problem. It is further a widely supported result of research on fear of crime that the level increases with age and that old women have the highest level while they have in reality the lowest risk of becoming a victim of a crime.

Heinz and Spiess found that citizens have feelings of insecurity in particular in the center of cities 40%. 10 percent of the citizens have feelings of insecurity in city parks and 8% at train stations in cities. Other places do not play a major role or cannot be defined. Their findings support what Wikstroem calls "hot spots". Wikstroem could identify in Stockholm hot spots which were peaceful during the day and very insecure in the late night and on weekends. Problem and community oriented policing could be the answer to control such hot spots and by the implementation of little preventive measures they could probably be made safe places. Whether this would change the feelings of security of the citizens has to be seen.

The majority of the citizens of Ravensburg/ Weingarten are in favour of more frequent police patrols in their neighbourhoods and this wish is increasing with age and independent of the gender of the citizens. While close to 60 percent of the male citizens age 14 to 19 favour more frequent police patrols, increases the percentage to just over 70 percent for the age group 65 and older. Quite similar looks the percentages for the females which went from 55 percent to just above 70 percent. If one takes into consideration the results of the study in Unna one can be quite sure that the citizens of Ravenburg/Weingarten would also prefer more foot and bicycle patrols and not police car patrols. This again would go hand in hand with the postulates of problem and community oriented policing.

The call for more presence of the police was also confirmed in the study of Murck. The citizens also asked for more police-community relations. Overall supported the citizens the principles of community and problem oriented policing and were not asking so much for harsher and tougher measures in the fight against crime. Very similar results reported also Heinz and Spieß for the cities of Ravensburg/Weingarten where the citizens were asking for better leisure time programs for juveniles and all sorts of measures to improve life in the cities rather than relying on harder measures in the fight against crime. The citizens favoured social measures as the best way to reduce feelings of insecurity and fear of crime . These results clearly indicate that the concepts of problem oriented and community policing to a certain degree reflect what the citizens expect and want from their police force even though the results are far from being clear and conclusive.

We did find in the evaluated surveys support for the notion that the citizens view the concepts of problem and community oriented policing in a favourable way. We further detected that the expectations of the citizens to a certain degree reflect what problem and community oriented policing postulate. However, since the concepts are at this moment not sufficiently operationalised one could argue that we can get under the umbrella of problem and community oriented policing everything which is new in the police work. Therefore we agree partly with Bayley who concludes that one will never know whether community policing will be successful since problem and community policing means too many things to different people.

The practice varies so much that any evaluation will be completely challengable or at least in part of not representing what problem and community oriented policing postulate. A central question seems to be in the case of problem and community oriented policing that we do not have anymore a clear role for the police: are the duties of the police to combat crime or are they supposed to work like a socialworker? If anything in between seems suitable: what is the appropriate mixture and how could individual police officers combine the very divergent competences needed to fullfill the different tasks? In the case of problem oriented policing are the police supposed to identify the main problems of certain groups in the population and to help solving them. However, population groups are not homogenous units and different groups identify problems different and also suggest different ways to solve them. Even if the police would be able to acknowledge the various sources of trouble it would often be impossible to find an agreement on how to solve them when the police are forced to work together with different subgroups and organisations in a given community. This would lead improve to a certain degree the feelings of security on the one hand, but would also lead to resignation and frustrations on the other hand for some of the residents who do not approve the suggested strategies in order to solve the problems.

The concepts and the combination of problem and community oriented policing sound very good in theory and might work quite well in countries which adhere to the opportunity principle. They still sound good in theory for countries with the legality principle. In countries with the legality principle are the police obliged by procedural law to enter prosecution in every case where exists preliminary suspicion that a crime was committed and to report it to the prosecutors office. Therefore the concepts are doomed and would probably fail even before one would start to implement them into practice.

The central part of problem and community oriented policing is that the relationship between the police officers and the citizens should be improved. This implies that when a police officer wants to built a trustworthy relationship with citizens in order to have a better understanding of the problems of the community he/she will hear about situations and events which are in a strict sense according to the laws illegal. In countries with the legality principle this would have the consequence that the police officer would have to report this "confidential knowledge" of a crime to the prosecutors office since the police have in general no discretion whatsoever and have to leave the final decision about to prosecute or to drop the charge to the prosecutors office.

In order to built up a trustworthy relationship, which is essential to problem and community oriented policing, the police officer has to have at least some discretion on how to react when he is informed about acts which constitute according to the laws a crime or are at the borderline. If the officer is forced to report the pettiest offences eventually to the prosecutors office one cannot expect that he will built up a meaningful relationship with any given community. Discretion and flexibility in how to interpret certain situations for police officers seem to be the essential parts if one wants to implement problem and community oriented policing in a community. If one takes these postulates seriously the concepts cannot function in countries with the legality principle unless they fundamentally change their penal procedural law.

Despite this specific problem for countries with the legality principle summarises Lustig rightly that the philosophy of community policing will in any system be defined by the fact that through the implementation of community and problem oriented policing neither the strategy of the police work, nor the logic of guaranteeing security, nor the power of the state will be changed. These three positions will be strengthened through the concepts of community and problem oriented policing, thus leading eventually to a netwidening effect. While this is basically true, indicate the results of views of citizens and citizens expectations that they are in favour of core elements of community and problem oriented policing and that through the implementation of these concepts the feelings of security and thus the quality of life can be improved for the citizens. Therefore netwidening effects are not necessarily negative unless they are used to control citizens in an intrusive way.

Some projects in the United States of America also support this conclusion, since they were able to reduce the number of crimes committed but even more important to reduce the fear of the citizens to become a victim of a crime. In addition they found in these projects that the level of satisfaction with the police was increased among the citizens. However, despite the reported success of these projects on local levels one has to be sceptical that the degree of satisfaction in a given population at large with the police work would overall improve.

In order to improve the general level of satisfaction with the police one would have to be able to show on a large scale that through measures of problem and community oriented policing the quality of life improved. The citizen by himself will hardly recognize a restructuring of the police force and the implementation of problem and community oriented policing unless it happens on a large scale, is continuously reported and favourably backed up by the media, or he gets directly involved. Scepticism is justified also by the fact that especially problem oriented policing is calling for solving the underlying problems of crime.

The experiences in the United States of America, where problem and community oriented policing was practiced and the relationship between the police, the citizens, and groups of the community was excellent and they all worked together, did not necessarily lead to solve problems of security and order in those communities. The reason for that is that the police cannot create jobs, improve the schools and get better teachers and often fails even to get the garbage collectors or street services better organised in order to improve the situation of a given community.

10

Education and Training for Urban Social Work

The development of professional social work can be divided into four epochs; 1880-1950 shapes the period of "the roots", the origin of a professional approach when attempts were made to construct and define own concepts and methods. The 1950s-1970s may be seen as the period of conflicts. The social workers fought between themselves about the question of working with individuals or on social matters, community work and politically, viewing these two lines as incompatible or antagonistic. During 1970-1990 the question of loyalty to the grass-roots ideology or professional, scientifically-based education came into focus.

Social work was defined as a semi-profession and there were enormous differences in the quality of the education and the status of social workers in the international perspective. Since the nineties social work is developing towards a more holistic profession, formulating definitions of common main goals and academic standards in education in the different countries and cultures. Now, in this fourth epoch, it seems of utmost importance for the profession to acknowledge the different views, the different approaches and methods thus guaranteeing solid professional standards.

Several researchers of the development of social work have stressed the importance of acknowledging the pluralistic nature of social work as well as both the generalist view and the need for expert knowledge in the age of competencies. Stressing the connection between theory and practice, policy and research is the other cornerstone for social work to build on today.

The different associations of social workers in the United States, in Canada and even in England have formed their special interest groups and associations around certain expert fields or specialist areas based on certain standards. Examples of these are social work in schools, social work in court, clinical/health social work, etc. It is now obvious - and actually may be a question of survival - to look at the diversities within the profession as a strength. Sven Hessle expresses this similarly:

> "Also, social work is contextual by nature, and this calls for an unbiased attitude and a constant willingness to negotiate in a range of a conflict-filled area of tension". Only such a standpoint will bring social workers an acknowledged and respectable status among other disciplines in the universities, among other professional categories and clients in the field and in society. It is in this context that the organisers of education have to work. To state this in another way: There are few doubts that an "intelligent" trade-off between field and research demands as well as between the specialised and the generalised profile is at the heart of the issue.

The Ministers of Education in the European countries have during the last decades been studying the structure and development of European higher education, stressing the universities' central role in developing European cultural dimensions. The Sorbonne declaration from May 1998 emphasized the creation of the European area of higher education "as a key way to promote citizens' mobility and employability and the continent's overall development". This perspective was already expressed in their Bologna Magna Carta Universitatum of 1988. There it was also stressed that European universities' independence and autonomy ensure that higher education and research systems continuously adapt to changing needs, society's demands and advances in scientific knowledge. This last sentence applies markedly to the basic assumptions of social work.

The work of the group of European Ministers mentioned above has been a process of describing, analysing and comparing higher education in general. This includes a project of providing an outline and overview of learning structures and a comparative analysis of the different systems embodying these structures. On the basis of this it has made recommendations for constructing a European area of higher education. The purpose should be achieving greater compatibility and comparability of the educational systems. Another important objective in this connection is increasing the European countries' international competitiveness. It is seen as necessary to ensure that the vitality and efficiency of any civilisation can be measured by the appeal that its culture and education has for other countries.

More concretely, the co-ordination of the European policy is thought to be implemented in reaching the following objectives in the new decade:

(a) an adoption of a system of easily readable and comparable degrees,

(b) an adoption of a system based on two main cycles, undergraduate,

(c) an adoption of a system of credits instead of expressing length of time and contents of study in terms of years or semesters making it more exchangable between countries,

(d) promotion of mobility for students, teachers, researchers and administrative staff. In this connection the co-ordination or the organisation of the academic studies in semesters is facilitating,

(e) promotion of co-operation in quality assurance,

(f) promotion of European dimensions regarding: curriculum development, inter-institutional co-operation, mobility schemes and integrated programmes of study, training and research.

These general demands are valid for all fields of education and a factor that must be dealt with also within social work education. There are also demands made for the social work education more specifically. In 1996 the Council of Europe presented a report of the analysing work of The Steering Committee on Social Policy which had worked on The initial and further training of social workers taking into account their changing role. Initially the authors of The Steering Committee stress the overall importance of empowering social work education in a changing Europe where "the pace of social and economic change has suddenly accelerated from a leisurely jog to a sprint.'

Inevitably, many of those who cannot keep up with the suddenly accelerated pace, or who are trampled down by it, end up in contact with the profession of social work. That is as it should be: because that is one of the primary reasons why this profession exists. Yet, the profession of social work is not a variety of magic; often its practitioners and those who educate them are nearly as disoriented as anyone else. In fact, sometimes social workers are even more disoriented and frightened than the general public, because they experience more quickly than most the gap between social reality and the institutional and financial arrangements which society provides to deal with it".

Phases of Social Work Education

It is argued within the International Association of Schools of Social Work (IASSW) that calling for minimum standards might lead to a development that lessens ambitions and makes them maximum standards. It is therefore feasible that the term minimum be left out altogether. The debate within the IASSW also clearly advocated that the general document to be produced by the IASSW should be accompanied by national or regional standards. The document should serve as a means for global compatibility, but not as a means for oppression of national and regional diversity.

In the report from the Steering Committee mentioned above the similarities and diversities of the education of social work in 24 countries was described and analysed. A striking gap was found between the different countries. All the Nordic countries were included in the study and it may be surprising for the European reader to see how different they are when compared, although belonging to the same Nordic welfare society and a closely related cultural area. This will also be evident in the coming presentation of traits and trends in the Nordic countries.

The Northeastern Association of Student Social Workers (NASSW) initiated in 1964 has the main purpose to enhance the education of social work in the Nordic countries through co-operation and exchange of experience and educational programmes. This Committee has worked with the opening question of comparability of the education for some time. This chapter attempts to present some aspects and arguments for working at a more integrated or even standardised structure of social work education. From a more specific point of view, it is aimed to specify a platform for discussions. Much of this concerns the problem of commensurability between a vocationally based orientation with ties to universities and an academic orientation with ties to the field. This further relates to the issue of a choice between educating either specialists or generalists.

There is no coherent model of social work education in the Nordic countries. Although belonging to the same regional and cultural area the development, policy and current status of the schools are quite different. The basis for these differences has of course historic roots and socio-cultural explanations.

The education in Denmark and Norway is oriented towards vocational training and is less than 4 years long. The teaching staff with scientific skills is mainly recruited from the social sciences with specialised competence from the diversified non-social work departments. The overwhelming majority of the teaching staff has practiced social work and the overwhelming percentage of these also present merits of post-graduate educational training. We could characterise it as the Specialised Field Model of education when describing its orientation. Its main benefit is the multi-dimensional approach to special social problems and phenomena.

The education is positioned outside the university system or with loose ties to it. The academic teaching staff face the demand to encompass knowledge of social work into their other academic profiles as political scientists, sociologists etc. The professionals with acquired field knowledge have a strong position in the model and the view of research is to tie it close to fieldwork, where normative issues are often raised. At the same time the connection to research is made secondary to the field relevance of the education. In this model the teachers are in the first place teachers of social work and then become researchers. The relation to the field is basically a bottom-up perspective and its demands on the curricula are pronounced and discussed from this perspective.

In contrast to this model Finland, Iceland and Sweden could be positioned under the Integrated Research Model. This indicates that they are leaving the traditional model. Such education shows some other distinct features. Education is tied more closely or belongs to the university system and the academic emphasis is stronger. This is also shown in the length of study, which is positioned more clearly in relation to the length of academic career programs. This educational model is striving at, and in some cases already attaining, an identity in its own academic subject Social Work. In this model teachers are to an increasing extent recruited on the basis of their academic merits in social work. To the extent that the traditional social sciences subjects are relevant to education the demand on the teachers goes the other way around, i.e. skills in social work have to be extended to skills in sociology, political science, etc. In this model lecturers are in the first place researchers, or experts in some core areas of social work, and secondly teachers. The relation to the field is turned around to become more top-down. This should be understood partly through the idea of academic freedom, and also from a more sceptical view towards the demands from the field for normative research – the norm rather becomes a demand for critical research. This has led to new challenges to the processing of experiences of field practice.

Also the teachers with basically field knowledge in the education are meeting increasing demands of having academic merits above their graduation as socionoms and the formal demands on new teachers move away from merits of knowledge and skills in practical social work to knowledge and skills in theoretical social work. While the former model had the ideal of professionally-focused work penetrating education, this model finds its rationale in education penetrating professionally-focused work.

This can be summarised in the following stylised way:

The Specialised Field Model	The Integrated Research Model
Education profile	Education profile
Vocational – BA	University degree – BA/MA/PhD
Shorter	Longer
Personal development	Academic training
Specific job positions	Broad work enrollment
Linked with other programs	Specific
researchers-Teachers	teachersàResearchers
Relation to field	Relation to field
Bottom-up	Top-down
UsefulCritical	
Friendship	Mutual scepticism
Relation to government	Relation to government
Labour market demand - Planning	Academic autonomy - Freedom

This model approach is of course a stylised one. The limitations of reality face elements of both models. Still there are some insights to be gainedfrom sketching such sharp contours. This is further the case since we firstly believe that general demands for change in Finnish, Icelandic and Swedish education have been in the direction of an Integrated Research Model. Much of these dynamics have been caused by the search for a core of social work as a major subject, which has been a strong demand within research. The importance of autonomous research in social work is emphasized by a number of those Nordic researchers and educational administrators who have written about the professional development of social work, its identity and differentiation from / cooperation with other disciplines.

We can further note that the other two countries Denmark and Norway are showing signs of breaking away from the old model and moving towards the other model, with increased demands for research affiliation. However, a process approach indicates primarily that shifts in models are always done at a specific time under specific circumstances and that a shift at a later point may imply omitting to copy less successful parts in the early movers' design. This opens the door for a new analysis of what is and ought to go on, with steps that are both alike and non-alike.

Let us first sketch out some specific advantages of the two models before we proceed to this issue:

- The Specialised Field Model
- High legitimacy in the professional field.
- Focus on the student's personal development.
- Students' acquired abilities directly useful to specific social work positions.
- The Integrated Research Model
- Critical and theorised outlook on social work from an autonomous position.
- Improved professional status and increased capability of taking part in debating social issues.
- Moving towards a better paid profession.

Looking at these points they, certainly to some extent, should not be seen as antagonising features in a combined education/research model for Social Work. Rather they comprise the essential features of an idealised model. Let us provisionally call it the Integrated Field Model. This model is at the center of some trends that can be used as the common platform. Using the term integrated model relates to the fact that the move towards a coherent platform of Social Work as an academic base, and skills of the academic professionals as well, is a key word for curriculum development. The notion of integration here is used to subsume the research orientation. The use of the term field model suggests that a high legitimacy in relation to the field is important – a relation that the Specialised Field Model should not lose and the Integrated Research Model to some extent has to re-conquer.

	Social sciences		Social work
Field	Denmark Norway		
		Integrated Field Model	
Research			Finland Iceland Sweden

This brings us to place the Integrated Field Model at the middle point in the chart above. It leaves with two different challenges for the member countries. For Denmark and Norway it demands that a reflexive academisation take place. The term reflexive suggests that what is brought in from the Integrated Research Model should be questioned and evaluated thoroughly in the process of breaking up. One example that this process is already on its way is given in Norway. Through his article "The Struggle around the Identity of Social Work" professor Pär Nygren initiated a debate on identity and research trying to convey that a platform for social work research should be formulated in Norway.

On the other hand Finland and Sweden might have to redefine their relation to the field and make a partial retreat. Let us talk of this process as a process of responsive cooperation. This new trade-off positioned in the middle should be seen not only as an idealised version but also as a realistic apprehension of ongoing trends in education; the most modern ones. It is also close to actual trends seen in all of the Nordic countries, however, being initiated from different positions. Today words like evidence-based social research and knowledge-based social work as well as competence-based education unfold new closer ties between research and the fields which are at the core of the Integrated Field Model as it is defined here. This meets the demands of the Steering Committee for "a high quality of theoretical education as well as practical training".

But it is just not evident in a new discourse and through the rhetoric. A new cooperation between research/education and the field is a dominant feature of changes taking place in the Nordic countries in a sort of corporatist model. The foundation of the Nordic FORSA collaboration which now has been established in all the Nordic countries may be seen as a catalyst in the development of a common scientific platform. Its conjoint research seminars have served as a forum for highlighting fruitful endeavours and various research activities. Further, the Nordic Forsa serves as a meeting place for researchers and practitioners, thus empowering a more theoretically-based professional identity in Nordic social work.

A characteristic feature of the development of social work education in Finland is the belief in institutionalised coordination– within the education system as well as in relation to the field. This is seen, for example, in the establishment of SOSNET - a network for collaboration between the universities in, for example, granting and coordinating the different specialisations in the PhD and licentiate programs. As to the relation to field work a new concept is brought in through the building up of so- called Competence Centers. The establishment of these centers is the result of an investigation initiated by the Social and Health Care Ministry in 1999. The first nine centers already constructed have been economically favoured and are now rapidly developing. The centers will, in their aim to tie practice closer to research and education, offer both appraisals of public programs and additional professional training as a development of practice teaching– also on a clinical basis. This development is also seen in Denmark and Norway. In accordance with suggestions in a resent evaluation of the Danish social work education the Danish Ministry of Education acknowledged in 2002 a reform including inter alia an extension of the study programme from 3 to 3 1/2 years with social work as a core subject qualifying for a Bachelor degree. The education in connection with the Ministry of Education in Denmark is also planning for a second stage platform to be worked out. This is to be coordinated through Centers for Further Education (CVU). These centers should be multi-disciplinary across the social, health and pedagogical sciences. The centers will open the door for the schools to join the academic environment and speed up the process of acquiring research competences in building up expertise within social work. The CVUs besides forming a new dialogue and solution with new partner, also should be viewed as a part of Danish reflexive academisation.

The latest evaluation of social work education in Sweden showed reflections around a move towards the Integrated Field Model. It was stated: "In contrast to what is often brought up as a critique of the social work programs the evaluation does not indicate a lack of scientific knowledge or familiarity with relevant research as a feature of the programs. Rather, the professional aspects are the critical points". More precisely, the contents of the education are directed towards 'personal development' and self-awareness, and philosophical and ethical reflections should be developed further. Furthermore, a new social work experimental education entity is planned in Sweden, where the ties between local communities and the education should be very close, also as regards research. In Iceland a four year social work study program is situated at the University of Iceland. It is closely linked within the faculty of social sciences but constructed as an autonomous core subject. It has strong research orientation but linked with the field. There is an increasing demand from the field to enhance the theoretical knowledge and skill to prepare students for professional responsibility in specialised social work areas.

The idea that there are some strong tendencies for the Nordic education models in the countries to move towards the Integrated Field Model is also strengthened if one recognises a last strong tendency. This is the tendency of related education programs to line up under the umbrella of a broadened but enhanced concept of Social Work. In the Swedish case the more professional education of social care is integrated with the social work education. Social Work is broadened as the "parent" discipline, while in Norway the tendency is that Social Work is enhanced as the "parent" discipline for the social, pedagogic and health orientations. In the Netherlands, at the school in Utrecht, the education is today positioned as belonging to the Specialised Field Model. This enhancement is now an outspoken strategy. The first point in their strategic development plan talks of a "growing cooperation between several types of education for social professions into a more cohesive social work approach". This implies that there is a tendency for Social Work to become a stronger discipline in itself not only through defining a research area but also through a new position in education. This, however, also leads to an example of how far the standardisation task should be brought. In this tendency of convergence there seem to be two education models for achieving the new integration with dominance for Social Work. This is seen in Sweden where the social work orientation and the social care orientation will have a common base and end in specific and differing in-depth studies, i.e. an opening model, while the school at Utrecht in their strategic plan discuss a closing model.

The coordination of their three distinct orientations - social work, social pedagogy and cultural and social education - is to be incorporated in their curriculum by starting with the specific and ending under the broad heading of an enhanced Social Work concept. The two models suggest that at the moment there are two trends – either starting with the broad and moving to the specific, or starting with the specific and moving to the broad. Also that the different approaches should be understood by tracing the line-up under Social Work to two different starting points. This meets the demands of the Steering Committee for "the self-understanding of social work as a profession and science" as a key factor.

Endeavours to Enhance Social Work Education

The IASSW has stated requirements to be fulfilled to become a member of the organisation. In the World Guide to Social Work Education from 1973 and from 1984 the requirements of the education programs are listed. The program must have the objective of preparation for social work; at least two years; include theoretical as well as field practice; have full-time staff members and full-time students; have a library and available teaching material; students should be selected on the basis of defined admissions requirements related to the academic standards of the program; assessment for a qualifying award should be based on all aspects of students' performance in the educational program.

From another point of view, the guide also serves the purpose of providing information necessary to identify differences in national educational systems and the patterns and content of social work education. By providing this type of factual information it also facilitates comparative study of the education and of its development over time, and may thus serve as a first basis for creating general standards for the education on an international level

The IASSW and CSWE (Council on Social Work Education) now publish on the one hand Educational Policy and Accreditation Standards (EPAS) last edition by CSWE 2001, and on the other hand we have the Handbook of Social Work Education. From these publications it is easy to see how strongly standards are stressed and although diversities are acknowledged the requirements for quality of any educational programme are described. It should, of course, be recognised that the pressure on schools and their organisations to form an opinion is obvious since external actors certainly have been concerned to make such demands on the education.

As early as 1967, The Committee of European Ministers made a resolution on the Role, training and status of Social Workers emphasising the importance of: recruiting an increased number of well-trained social workers to meet the new and constantly changing needs; stressing the close interdependence between the function, the training and the status of social workers. In order to fulfil the international definition of social work: "social work is a specific professional activity which aims at favouring a better mutual adaptation of individuals, families, groups and the social environment in which they live, and developing the self-respect and self-responsibility of the individual, utilising the capacities of persons, interpersonal relations and resources provided by the community" and practice social work professionally the following recommendations were made: In each country a study of the functions of social workers should be kept under review and further developed; regarding the complexity of human problems and the interdependency of their components it is important to work in contact with other professions; focus should be on the preventive as well as remedial aspects of the different branches of social work as better knowledge helps to avoid difficult problems; social workers should be responsible for helping communities to initiate services; social workers should participate in social research; social workers should contribute to the development of social policy, pointing out needs and giving opinions on means designed to meet them; social workers should play a constructive role in the implementation of social measures at both central and local level.

In the quoted resolution there are also a number of recommendations on "The goals of the schools of social work" and how to ensure the quality of the education, i.e. the following: Governments should consider adequate equipment for the schools of social work, which possibly calls for training at various levels; curricula should cover the same body of knowledge; as practical training is essential. Governments should encourage social agencies and institutions to contribute by providing facilities for ensuring supervised practical training; sufficient number of both full-time and part-time teachers; a period of general training ought to precede specialisation of social workers; linking advanced training with the universities.

Finally the resolution touches on "The status of social workers". Among other things mentioned are measures to be taken to protect the respective titles of professionally trained social workers; granting them career advancement and fair salaries; they should enjoy a high degree of independence in performance of the professional functions; the delicate and confidential nature of social work should be recognised and respected by the employer; Governments should favour measures and developments that may enable social workers to take employment in the territory of another European member country.

With regard to the described social changes, it is pointed out that the strong expectations for social workers to solve severe social problems with minimal resources are unrealistic now. Also, it is pointed out, "the usually too heavy caseload is not met with enough professional support and opportunities for further development". Thus, only social workers who are furnished with efficient and appropriate professional tools, achieving respect and being honoured by the society, are able to deal with the issues that are indisputably on the agenda of post-cold war Europe. This means, the authors claim, that only academic education consisting of solid theoretical knowledge, training in the field and developed self-understanding will make social workers of the future.

Also modern authorities in social work have entered the debate. In a new publication on "International Standard-setting of Higher Social Work Education" Malcolm Payne also outlines how social workers can use different means to identify and maintain standards. First, he points out that the tradition in social work of critical reflection and internal debate towards improvement makes social work as a profession academically, personally and professionally satisfying. Second, he points out the importance of written requirements or statements about social work in shaping its own standards instead of getting them from elsewhere. Third, as social workers are a part of the local, national and international academic community, being in communication is inevitable, and to some extent in competition, with one another. Fourth, some kind of external scrutiny serves as a support in keeping up standards or keeping sight of acknowledged goals. One way of forming professional standards is working on them as a process, e.g. by examining the students' process from intake to graduation.

Before turning to the closing remarks on compatibility and comparability we have to clearly state once again that ideas of standardisation and variation have to be defined with care. Social work is a socially constructed activity. With that in mind the development of social work education has to allow for a certain amount of regional autonomy and diversity while regarding common professional and ethical standards.

As to compatibility the term is closely related to common standards. Compatibility is much associated with free movement of students, teachers as well as professionals. It must be built up around the international definition of Social Work as a basis for curricula and research areas. The idea of compatabilty will lead us to discussing similar or coordinated guidelines and procedures for intake as well as common grading scales and common education skills to be promoted.

Comparability allows for diversity and difference. It requires, however, that differences should be transparent and have basic components of similarity within them. Basic issues such as protection of the professional title and its contents as well as accreditation rules of schools must, if not brought to coherence among the Nordic countries, be clearly stated to allow for comparability. The demand for increased professionalisation and academisation of social work education in the Nordic countries follows at the moment two different lines of thought. Denmark and Norway at the moment work towards a 3+2 year professionally oriented basic and furthering education as a standard, while Iceland, Finland and Sweden argue for a 4 year academic professional education with strong research orientation. It is probably hard to come to one solution regarding this in the near future, not least because the differences are rooted in different historical contexts. We should, however, understand that differences might also convey similarity. This means that even two prototypes of this kind can contain and should contain some basic components that at least reveal some minimum common standards. It should be noted that the modern instrument of quality assurance will help to serve as a tool in any discussions on standardisation, and is a major instrument in allowing for comparability.

Education for Urban Child Welfare

Considerable attention has been given in the literature to the goal of reprofessionalising public child welfare services in the United States. Primary focus has addressed the need for better-educated and trained front-line child protection workers while government and nongovernment organisations as well as accrediting bodies have endorsed social workers as ideal for child welfare supervisors.

Social work, as a profession, has taken a lead role in this endeavor by advocating for the employment of professional social workers in public child welfare agencies. The use of Title IV-E funds to prepare social work students for careers in public child welfare has reinforced the status of social work as a lead influence in structuring the labor pool for public child welfare agencies in many regions of the United States. There are isolated findings that assert that master's of social work (MSW) students attain better outcomes with clients than those with bachelor degrees (BSW), Title IVE stipend recipients are more knowledgeable and skilled in child welfare practice than others, and that social work–educated workers remain in public child welfare longer than others.

However, many of these findings are generated from studies with limited rigor, nonrepresentative (i.e., nonrandom) samples, and with few comparisons among those child welfare workers with varied educational and training experiences. Furthermore, the influence of the quality of supervision received was not a controlling influence in many of these studies. This is an important consideration given recent attention and findings in the child welfare field that emphasize the positive influence of good supervisory skills (and relationships with workers) on the recruitment and retention of child welfare workers. These findings highlight the importance of the supervisor and the need for a quality supervisory relationship for retaining quality child welfare staff. There is an abundance of literature that highlights the skills and knowledge considered representative of a good supervisor or manager in the human service fields, including child welfare. Social work educators and researchers typically endorse the MSW degree as preferred for those assuming supervisor and/or management positions in child welfare and social service agencies.

These endorsements seemed to be based on the historical role of social work in educating and training professionals to assume supervisory and administrative roles in social service agencies. What is less convincing is the extent to which a social work degree enhances the skills of those that assume supervisor positions in contrast to those without a social work degree. In an isolated study, evaluations of field supervisors with MSW degrees and those with a master's or doctorate in another human service profession, revealed that "there are no meaningful differences in the quality of field instruction supervision" provided by supervisors with a MSW or other professional graduate degree.

A recent study considered supervisory evaluations across all fields of practice as such pertains to field supervision. It is not known, and there is limited research that examines, if the performance of child welfare supervisors varies according to different educational backgrounds and training. The study compared and contrasted the ratings on 30 measures of performance of a representative sample of child welfare supervisors in Florida with different educational backgrounds who received performance evaluations in March 2002. It was conducted in accordance with one of a number of recommendations of a Blue Ribbon Panel formed in Florida under Executive Order 02-159 by Governor Bush.

The study compared the job performance of child welfare supervisors with degrees in social work, other behavioral science degrees, and other non-humanservice degrees using existing data collected from the Florida Department of Children and Families (DCF). The DCF informed the author of the number of supervisors employed in March 2002 throughout Florida.

Given the terms of the contract and Institutional Review Board (IRB) approved protocol, the author did not have access to any identifying demographic data/ information associated with each supervisor nor any client/case data. The DCF officials were responsible for collecting performance evaluations from district offices and providing the author only with a hardcopy of the performance ratings and educational degree of each supervisor included in the study.

The number of supervisors in Florida (at the time of the study) included 180 child protective investigator (CPI) supervisors and 212 family service counselor and/or child protective service (CPS) supervisors. Of these, performance evaluations apparently existed for 133 CPI supervisors and 166 CPS supervisors. By way of explanation, these individuals (which constitute the sampling frame) were employed at least 6 months in their current position and/or class title.

Those employed fewer than 6 months would not have received a performance evaluation in March 2002. A decision was made by the author to request the evaluation reports of all 299 supervisors that constituted the population of supervisors that received a performance evaluation in March 2002. DCF officials requested all supervisor evaluations from district offices. In total, 175 supervisors or 58.5% of all supervisors with at least 6 months experience were received. There was no formal stated reason given for the nonreceipt of select performance evaluations. The response rate differed considerably across regional service districts in a manner that was statistically significant. No supervisor evaluations were received from District 10. Among those service regions and/or districts that did participate, response rates varied from a low of 28.6% to a high of 100%.

The number of supervisors employed in each service district or region varies in accordance with the size of the service area (in population and demand for service) and resources. Although there was variance in the response rate across service districts, a response rate of 80% or higher was received from districts and/or regions employing 50.1% of all CPI and CPS workers, serving an aggregate total of 61.85% of all in-home and out-of-home care cases, and investigating 55.68% of all maltreatment allegations in Florida in 2002.

Given the interest in comparing supervisor evaluations according to educational background, representatives from Human Resources at DCF surveyed every supervisor and requested that he or she update and/or correct any discrepancies in information pertaining to their educational background (degrees received and the disciplines and/or major associated with each). Confirmation of educational background was received from 271 of the population of supervisors throughout Florida. Among those for which performance evaluations were received (n = 175), educational background could not be confirmed for 12 (6.8%) of the sample. These evaluations would be excluded from key analyses. CPI and CPS worker supervisors have varied professional backgrounds.

The listing of educational majors and degrees and/or levels obtained are ranked according to the number of supervisors contained in each category. Among the population of supervisors, 35 educational majors are represented. The education majors most represented include social work, psychology, education, sociology, criminology, and business. These majors constitute 18.1%, 12.0%, 11.4%, 11.4%, 8.3% and 4.7%, respectively, of the total population. It is interesting to note, these 6 educational majors parallel the educational majors most represented among CPI and CPS workers in Florida.

However, unlike CPI and CPS workers (where those with psychology degrees are the modal group), supervisors with degrees in social work are the modal group within the population and sample of supervisors participating in the study. Although the response rate to the study was 58.5%, the proportion of supervisors in the sample with different educational degrees closely resembles the proportionate distribution found in the population.

In an additional attempt to gauge the representative nature of those supervisors included in the study, comparisons were made between those supervisors included versus excluded from the sample in terms of years of experience in the DCF and amount of experience prior to assuming the current position and/or title of child welfare supervisor. By way of explanation, the researcher was provided the hire date for each participant and the date she or he was appointed to her or his current title of supervisor.

Table 1

Distribution of Study Cases in Sampling Frame, and Final Sample by Educational Major and/or Background of Supervisors

Educational Major Sampling Frame (N)	*Percentage in in Final*	*Percentage Sample (n)*
Social work	18.1 (54)	16.6 (29)
Psychology	12.0 (36)	13.7 (24)
Sociology	11.4 (34)	9.7 (17)
Education	11.4 (34)	12.0 (21)
Criminology	8.3 (25)	8.0 (14)
Business action	4.7 (14)	6 9 (12)
Other27.1 (81)	26.3 (46)	
Missing	7.0 (21)	6.9 (12)
Totals	100 (299)	100 (175)

These dates, in combination with the date of the primary evaluation permitted the computation (in years and months) that a supervisor was a DCF employee (as a worker and supervisor) and the length of time as an employee prior to being appointed a supervisor. In terms of total time of service, those included in the sample had a mean number of 11.40 years (SD = 7.47) years of experience, with a median of 10.1 years of experience (range between 1 and 30.25 years). Those excluded from the sample had mean number of 11.36 years (SD = 8.05) years of experience, with a median of 9.13 years of experience (range between 6 months and 35.17 years). An independent t test revealed no significant differences between those supervisors included versus excluded from the sample in terms of the number of years employed by DCF ($t = -.045$, $df = 297$, $p = .964$) and the number of years experience between original hire and current assignment of supervisor ($t = -.987$, $df = 297$, $p = .324$). Thus, there appears to be no difference in those included versus excluded from the sample in terms of educational backgrounds and the years of experience as a DCF employee and child welfare supervisor.

Like the workers they supervise, the vast majority (76.6%) of child welfare supervisors in Florida possess a bachelor's degree as their highest educational level. Among the remaining supervisors, 15.4% have a graduate degree, 3.0% received some graduate education (without attainment of a degree), 1.7% had a PhD, JD, or MD, 1% had an associate's degree, and 1% had a high school diploma. Among those evaluations received (that are part of the sample), there are a slightly higher proportion (78.3%) and a slightly lower proportion (12.0%) that have a bachelor's and master's degree (respectively) than observed in the population.

Additional examination reveals that in the population of supervisors, those with social work degrees constitute 32.6% of all those with master's degrees. Following social workers, those with a major in education are most represented (15.2%) among those with graduate degrees. Only two supervisors with backgrounds in business and criminology had graduate degrees. One person had a graduate degree in psychology, and there were no supervisors with master's degrees in sociology. Given the small proportion of supervisors with graduate degrees, analyses focused on comparisons between supervisors based on their educational majors and/or backgrounds regardless of educational level obtained.

Performance Evaluation

Child welfare supervisors were rated using two assessment tools. These include the Management Performance Evaluation Form and a Peer Input Form. These tools measure the performance of supervisors using standardised performance expectations that attempt to capture the multitude of skills needed to provide quality service as a public employee. The Management Performance Evaluation Form is completed by each supervisor's immediate supervisor and/or administrator, typically a district administrator for the DCF. The Peer Input Form is completed typically by fellow unit supervisors, administrators, or other individuals "who are familiar with the [supervisor's] performance, work products and/or services".

For each form, raters were requested to score each supervisor on individual performance items using a Likert-type scale anchored in the following manner:

1 Performance is inadequate, below minimum acceptable standards, expectations, and objectives. Performance is causing problems, inconvenience, or hardship for coworkers or the department and is having a negative impact on productivity or service. Performance should not be continued at this level. Additional training or behavioral adjustments required.

2 Performance marginally meets requirements at expected level. Improvement is needed and expected. Compared to others with similar responsibilities, the employee requires more frequent supervisory direction to accomplish assigned tasks. Performance at this level is "just getting by."

3 Performance consistently meets and occasionally exceeds expectations. Produces the type of quality

work expected from a qualified person. Performance at times may be higher or lower but average to the competent level.

4 Performance consistently meets and often exceeds expectations. Performance is characterised by initiative and superior job knowledge. Actively contributes to the achievement of overall goals. Performance is recognised by peers.

5 Performance significantly exceeds all expectations on a regular basis and is not generally equaled by others in the same position. Performance at this level is recognised by peers, immediate supervisors, and others in the agency and/or department. Actively initiates improvements and fosters teamwork. Extremely capable in adjusting priorities to current needs. Effective communicator. Works well independently for the good of the agency.

6. No longer applicable or unable to determine.

Unlike the CPI and CPS workers, supervisors were rated on more standardised expectations. Here, each supervisor was rated on 12 organisational efficiency, productivity, and effectiveness expectations, and 8 individual efficiency, productivity, and effectiveness expectations. These 20 performance expectations are considered "critical elements" of supervisors' performance. In addition to these 20 critical elements, supervisors were rated on one standardised performance expectation labeled "Performance Expectation #1" that is worded in the following manner:

> Employee is expected to demonstrate, model and reinforce the agency's values of fairness, cooperation, respect, commitment, honesty, excellence, and teamwork and state fundamental values of fairness, cooperation, respect, commitment, excellence, and honesty. The standard to be applied for this expectation is that the employee demonstrated these values the vast majority of the time in

their interactions with co-workers, supervisors, and customers; in the personal contributions to work assignments and projects; and when representing the agency or the state.

The standardised expectations of supervisors will be the focus of analyses for the study. A detailed list of the 20 critical elements and/or performance expectations of supervisors is as follows:

Organisational Efficiency, Productivity, and Effectiveness

- *Planning:* Bases plans on department missions and goals with a thorough analysis of relevant facts, justifies cost and benefits, sets realistic goals and schedules.
- *Controlling:* Develops performance or quality control standards, measures results, takes corrective actions and resolves performance problems.
- *Organising:* Arranges work for the most efficient handling and eliminates unnecessary activities, operates efficiently.
- Results planning and/or achievement: Plans organisational goals and standards and establishes measurement criteria, uses monitoring procedures to review progress, achieves planned goals in a timely manner.
- *Work products:* Produces reports, correspondence, and other work products that meet the intended objectives in a timely manner; demonstrates professional competency and reflects acceptable quality.
- *Budget management:* Maintains appropriate budgetary controls, monitors activities and initiates timely and effective corrective actions, stays within budget, makes appropriate budgetary recommendations.

- *Managing change:* Initiates change effectively and adapts to necessary changes in operations, motivates employees to have a positive attitude toward operational changes.
- *Directing leadership:* Sets challenging goals, delegates and coordinates effectively, promotes innovation in achieving goals, sets examples for subordinates.
- *Staffing:* Selects qualified people; matches employee skills and abilities with job requirements; assigns staff appropriately for workload; identifies, develops, and improves technical skills of subordinates.
- *Performance appraisal and/or feedback:* Effectively evaluates subordinates, encourages and initiates regular discussion of performance with subordinates, takes appropriate and timely action with marginal or failing performers, recognises and rewards good performance.
- *Discipline administration:* Uses corrective discipline to improve performance and/or behavioral problems.
- *Equal opportunity:* Actively supports and works toward fulfilling the agency's affirmative action efforts, recognises and coordinates the development and promotional opportunities for employees.

Individual Efficiency, Productivity, and Effectiveness

- *Problem analysis and/or decision making:* Analyses problems comprehensively,makes timely and practical decisions.
- *Technical skills:* Knowledgeable of methods, techniques, and skills required in own and/or related function(s); applies specific methods, procedures, and techniques in functional area.

— *Conceptual skills:* Conceptualises the organisation's relationship with other entities, understands organisational subunit relationships and dependencies, acts accordingly.

— *Presentations:* Develops clear, well-organised, and logical presentations; reduces complex issues to simple terms; sensitive to audience levels.

— *Self-direction:* Personally well-organised, uses time effectively, acts independently.

— *Self-motivation:* Motivated to succeed, extends personal resources, builds on strengths and works on deficiencies.

— *Human relation skills:* Communicates clearly and listens effectively, keeps others informed, deals effectively with conflict.

— *Relationships:* Develops and maintains effective working relationships with other departmental managers, state managers, legislature, media, service recipients, and the public.

These 20 critical elements provide an overview of skills and competencies frequently cited in the professional literature as necessary components for effective supervisory and/or administrative practice. For example, Tropman et al. classified key supervisory skills needed in child welfare as planning, training/coaching/teaching/educating/mentoring, supportive communication, working with workers (and others) with strong opinions, running effective meetings, decision making and/or problem solving, monitoring/reviewing/evaluating, and management of self. When these skills are operationalised, Tropman et al. asserted that planning involves the ability to work "with the worker proactively and reactively through a process of planning work, assuring [project or service] goals remain center stage" and outcomes are accomplished within established and reasonable time frames. It also includes functions associated with organising, strategising, staffing, budgeting, and overseeing.

Critical elements for supervisory practice (denoted on the Management Performance Evaluation Form) that mirror these functions include the following (associated with organisational efficiency, productivity, and effectiveness functions): planning, organising, results planning and/or achievement, budget management, staffing, and performance appraisal and/or feedback. Salas suggested the "core components of supervisory and management effectiveness" with CPS include skills and functions associated with communication, control, feedback, supervisory focus, production, as well as interpersonal skills. They also identified a number of "supervisory practices that assist in building and maintaining staff capacity, creating the foundation for unit performance, and establishing positive relationships with upper management".

These include practices associated with delegating, monitoring outcomes, giving feedback, supporting the emotional needs of staff, influencing others, analysing problems, making decisions, and managing conflict or mediating. These skills and practices are paralleled in the Management Performance Evaluation Form. For example, skills associated with "production" functions identified by Salas closely resemble those identified with "results planning and/or achievement" functions for which Florida child welfare supervisors are evaluated. Although the elements that supervisors are rated on are generally acknowledged as important, they do not specifically relate to child welfare service outcomes associated with the service units overseen by each supervisor. Please note that the administrator rating each supervisor may use a number of sources of information when making a determination and/or rating of a supervisor's performance. Unfortunately, these sources of information are not denoted on the evaluation forms, and the researcher did not have access to each rater to ask follow-up questions.

In addition to the Management Performance Evaluation Form and its measurement of performance on 20 "critical elements" of supervisory performance, feedback is solicited from the peers of each supervisor using the Peer Input Form. This form mirrors the Peer Input Form utilised with CPI and CPS worker evaluations.

The number of peers that evaluate each employee can vary according to the size of the county and/or service area and number of other supervisors and administrators each supervisor interacts with. Unfortunately, the titles and/or positions of each peer selected to rate a supervisor were not typically detailed on the peer input forms received by the researcher. Thus, it is not possible to conduct analyses that contrast the ratings of supervisors as such may be done by other supervisors of CPI and CPS workers, other junior-level administrators not supervising front-line workers, or senior administrators. Regardless, peer evaluations were received for 144 (82.3%) of the 175 supervisors that were included in the sample. The number of peers that evaluated each supervisor ranged between 1 and 9 with 91.7% (n = 132) of supervisors with peer ratings receiving an evaluation from at least five peers.

All of the performance expectations and the rating scale in the Peer Input Form are standardised. The specific items (and descriptors) for which someone rates their peer include:

1. *Teamwork:* Encourages and facilitates cooperation, pride, trust, and group identity; fosters commitment

and team spirit; works with others to achieve goals. Understands and demonstrates that individual success is dependent on the success of the team.

2. *Interpersonal skills:* Expresses information to individuals or groups effectively; listens to others and responds appropriately. Shows understanding, courtesy, tact, empathy, concern, and is sensitive to individual differences.

3. *Initiative:* Sets well-defined and realistic goals; displays a high level of initiative, effort, and commitment toward completing assignments in a timely manner; works with minimal supervision; is motivated to achieve; demonstrates responsible behavior.

4. *Planning and organising:* Organises work, sets priorities, determines resource requirements, coordinates with other units as necessary; meets deadlines.

5. *Flexibility and/or creativity:* Is open to change and new information; adapts behavior or work methods in response to new information, changing conditions, or unexpected obstacles; effectively deals with ambiguity. Uses creativity to develop new insights into situations and applies innovative solutions to problems.

6. *Customer service:* Works with internal and external customers to assess needs, provide assistance, resolve problems, satisfy expectations; knows the Department's mission and functions and operates effectively within them; is committed to providing quality customer service.

7. *Quality:* Is thorough when performing work and is conscientious about attending to detail; consistently performs work assignments on time with a high degree of accuracy.

8. *Leadership:* Influences, motivates, and challenges others; adapts leadership style to a variety of situations; sets challenging goals; delegates and coordinates effectively; sets examples for subordinates.
9. Supports and exemplifies the agency's values of fairness, cooperation, respect, commitment, honesty, excellence, and teamwork and state fundamental values of fairness, cooperation, respect, commitment, excellence, and honesty.

Ratings of Supervisors' Performance

The performance of supervisors is rated using a Management Performance Evaluation Form. Supervisors were rated on 20 performance expectations and one general standardised performance expectation labeled "Performance Expectation #1." The standardisation of expectations and the scale for evaluating performance on these expectations allows for meaningful comparisons of data across study groups. Supervisors were divided into study groups according to their educational background and/or major. A series of ANOVA procedures were utilised to examine if ratings across supervisors on each of the performance expectations varied significantly according to the educational background of the supervisor.

ANOVA procedures typically assume a balanced design. The greatest discrepancy affecting the balance of the design exists with the number of workers contained in the "all other majors" group (which is not of primary concern for the study given the multitude of different educational backgrounds represented in this group). Regardless, as a means of maximising the validity of the results garnered from ANOVA procedures, the following statistical procedures and/or process was engaged in:

random and fixed effects (ANOVA) models were computed; a Levene statistic was computed to test for homogeneity of variance; if variance estimates were equal (i.e., homogeneous), a Tukey's B and Bonferroni test were conducted in an attempt to gauge if the performance scores differed between any two groups of workers; given that the group sizes were unbalanced (i.e., unequal), harmonic means of group sizes were used for the Tukey's B test; if variance estimates (using the Levene statistic) were unequal, the Tamhane's T2 and Dunnett's C statistics were computed in an attempt to gauge if the performance scores differed between any two groups of workers.

Peer Evaluations

The peers of each supervisor provided an evaluation of the supervisor using a Peer Input Form. This form requested that the peer to rate his or her colleague on nine standardised performance items using a standardised 5-point scale.

Unfortunately, peer input forms were not received for 31 (17.7%) of 175 supervisors whose evaluations were examined for the study. DCF officials provided no explanation for the missing data. Analysis of peer data is limited to the 144 sampled workers for which Peer Input Forms were received; findings are qualified by this fact. Although the Peer Input Form provides instructions for calculating an "average rating" of a worker by each peer, the researcher compared workers (across educational backgrounds) using a variety of different mechanisms. First, instead of computing an average rating (on a scale from 1 to 5) across all individual peer average ratings, the researcher computed an average total peer evaluation score (with a range of 9 to 45).

This score had a larger range and, subsequently, allowed for greater variation in the performance evaluations of workers by their peers than using the score typically used by DCF officials in Florida. Summing all the total peer evaluation scores and dividing this summed score by the number of peers completing evaluations computed the average total peer evaluation score.

Furthermore, given that each performance item addressed a very specific item and/or performance measure, the average score for each individual item was computed for each worker, and these scores were compared across workers with different educational backgrounds. There were no significant differences in the performance evaluations of supervisors as rated by their peers with respect to skills and abilities associated with teamwork, interpersonal skills, initiative, planning and organisation, flexibility and/or creativity, customer service, general work quality, leadership, ability to support and exemplify their agency's values.

The study attempted to examine the extent to which the educational background of child welfare supervisors in Florida affected their performance as evaluated by their immediate superior and peers. Although an attempt was made to survey and receive the performance evaluations of all CPS and CPI supervisors in Florida, evaluations were received from 58.5% of all supervisors. Supplemental analyses suggest that respondents are representative of the broader population of supervisors in terms of educational backgrounds and the years of experience as a DCF employee and child welfare supervisor.

The performance evaluation scores did not differ among supervisors from different educational backgrounds for any of the individual standardised performance expectations examined in the study. Supervisors were evaluated using a Management Performance Evaluation Form on 20 critical elements and/

or performance expectations. Twelve of these elements addressed organisational efficiency, productivity, and effectiveness expectations. Another 8 of these elements focused on individual efficiency, productivity, and effectiveness expectations.

No statistically significant differences on each of the 20 performance expectations were observed in the ratings of supervisors with degrees in social work, psychology, sociology, education, criminology, business, or all other degrees (combined). When peer evaluations were considered there were no statistically significant differences in the performance evaluations of supervisors (with different degrees) as rated by their peers with respect to skills and abilities associated with teamwork, interpersonal skills, initiative, planning and organisation, flexibility and/or creativity, customer service, general work quality, leadership, ability to support and exemplify their agency's values.

Findings from the study suggest that the performance of child welfare supervisors does not vary and is not influenced by supervisors' educational background. Unfortunately, given that the vast majority of child welfare supervisors in Florida had a bachelor's degree, the study was unable (with any statistical power) to test assumptions endorsed in the literature that MSWs are the best qualified to serve as child welfare supervisors.

The endorsement of MSWs typically results from critical reviews of curricula in graduate school of social work and the applicability and relevance of these curricula to on-the-job demands and competencies required of child welfare supervisors. There is a dearth of rigorous studies that contrast the performance of supervisors with MSWs to those with other type and levels of academic degrees. Although the influence of level of degree could not be determined in the study, social work supervisors perform no better nor worse than nonsocial workers on 30 standardised performance measures as evaluated by their immediate superiors or peers.

The performance expectations examined in the study address skills and knowledge generally associated within the literature with quality supervisory and/or management practice in the social services and child welfare settings. Although clear distinctions are drawn within the literature between management and supervisory functions, Florida trained and prepared supervisors and managers (regardless of department) using the same standardised curricula. The skills learned in these trainings would be applied across a variety of contexts.

Although the performance expectations supervisors are evaluated on are numerous and detailed, the study did not examine supervisory skills and knowledge that may relate to the outcomes of specific child welfare practices. The standardised instruments do not detail any information regarding the quality of service delivered by supervisees and the level of influence their supervisory skills had on worker efficacy. Furthermore, there was no attempt in these evaluations to rate the knowledge and expertise of supervisors as such applies across different service contexts and with specific fields of child welfare practice (i.e., risk assessments, permanency and concurrent planning, reunification efforts, out-of-home care, etc.) for which they guide, mentor, advise, and evaluate the performance of front-line workers.

Although these specific functions may be embodied within performance expectations (in the Management Performance Evaluation Form) such as those identified as controlling, results planning and/or achievement, staffing, and performance appraisal and/or feedback skills, there is no explicit mention of the service contexts where these skills are exemplified. It is possible that a supervisor when "managing change" is very effective and competent when dealing with issues of permanency and concurrent planning but not so with issues associated with reunification efforts.

Although evaluators may have considered these issues and/or factors, such information was not collected on the evaluation form, and the researcher did not have access to the evaluators to survey them on the sources of information used when rating each supervisor on each critical element. Findings are qualified by these facts. Given such, a detailed stratification of evaluations across service contexts and/or issues in future studies on supervisor performance in child welfare would significantly contribute to the knowledge base on this topic. Although general competency-based standards are reinforced in a number of expectations for which supervisors are evaluated, there was no gauge of related knowledge important in guiding workers in casework decisions and interactions with child welfare clients.

Bibliography

Amis, P., "Making sense of poverty", in IIED, 1995, *Urban poverty: characteristics, causes and consequences,* Environment and Urbanization, Vol 7 No 1, 1995.

Browman, G. P., *Editorial: Development and aftercare of clinical guidelines: The balance between rigor and pragmatism, JAMA, 286*(12), 1509-1511, 2001.

Davies, Celia, *Gender and the Professional Predicament in Nursing,* Buckingham: Open University Press, 1995.

DiCenso, A., Cullum, N., & Ciliska, D., "Implementing evidence-based nursing: Some misconceptions", *Evidence-Based Nursing, 1(2),* 38-39, 1998.

Forsythe, B. and Jordan, B., "The Victorian Ethical Foundations of Social Work in England: Continuity and Contradiction", *British Journal of Social Work,* 32(7), pp.847-862, 2002.

Fustukian, S.,, "Strategies to strengthen urban health and social development", in N. Hall, R. Hart and D. Mitlin, *The Urban Opportunity: The Work of NGOs in Cities of the South,* London: ITDG, 1996.

Gambrill, E., "Social work: An authority-based profession", *Research on Social Work Practice, 11*(2), 166-175, 2001.

Geyman, J. P.,Deyo, R. A.,&Ramsey, S. D. (Eds.), *Evidencebased clinical practice: Concepts and approaches,* Boston: Butterworth Heinemann, 2000.

Gilbert, A., "Work and poverty during economic restructuring: the experience of Bogota, Colombia", *IDS Bulletin,* Vol 28 No 2, Brighton: Institute of Development Studies, 1997.

Gilligan, C., "Moral orientation and moral development", in V. Held (ed.) *Justice and Care: Essential Readings in Feminist Ethics.* Boulder, CO: Westview Press, 1995.

Healy, Karen, *Social Work Practices: Contemporary Perspectives on Change,* London: Sage, 2000.

Lyons, J.,&Khot, A., "Information in practice: Managing information overload: Developing an electronic directory", *British Medical Journal, 320,* 160, 2000.

Macleod, J., Gill, P., & Smith, G. D., *Evidence and primary care,* Lancet, *353,* 1621, 1999.

Neuman, B.,&Young, R. J., "A model for teaching total person approach to patient problems", *Nursing Research, 21,* 264-269, 1972.

Park K., *Park's Textbook of Preventive and Social Medicine,* 17th ed. Jabalpur: M/s Banarsidas Bhanot publishers; 2002.

Parton, N., "Some thoughts on the relationship between theory and practice in and for social work", *British Journal of SocialWork, 30,* 449-463, 2000.

Percheon D., Guest C. and Gray M., *Oxford Handbook of Public Health Practice,* Oxford : Oxford University Press, 2003.

Ruston, A., & Nathan, J., "The supervision of child protection work", *British Journal of Social Work, 26,* 357-374, 1996.

Salas, M., *Supervising child protective services caseworkers,* Washington, DC: U.S. Department of Health and Human Services, Administration for Children and Families, 2004.

Zlotnik, J., *Social work education and public human services: Developing partnerships,* Alexandria,VA: Council on Social Work Education, 1993.

Index